Also by Shawn Nevins

THE RESURRECTION OF JOHN DAVIS: A SCREENPLAY

THE CELIBATE SEEKER: AN EXPLORATION OF CELIBACY
AS A MODERN SPIRITUAL PRACTICE

ADVENTURES IN CAVING: KENTUCKY AND INDIANA

CW00951987

With Bob Fergeson

IMAGES OF ESSENCE

SUBTRACTION:

The Simple Math of Enlightenment

Shawn Nevins

TAT Foundation Press

Published by TAT Foundation Press
Thomas Green Road
Roxboro, North Carolina 27574

Text font: Palatino Linotype

Main entry under title: *Subtraction: The Simple Math of
Enlightenment*

Spirituality   2. Psychology

ISBN: 978-0-9864457-2-9
Library of Congress Control Number: 2017912696

Table of Contents

Foreword 7

The Prelude and the Purpose 13

Chapter 1: End of Life One. 17

Chapter 2: What Shall You Become? 31

Chapter 3: The Haunting Presence of Richard Rose . 49

Chapter 4: The Natural Koan 63

Chapter 5: Choose a Direction 73

Chapter 6: Outhouse Zen 85

Chapter 7: Goat Hugging 105

Chapter 8: I Will Take Leave of Thee 119

Chapter 9: Winter, Summer, Winter 133

Chapter 10: Into the World. 149

Chapter 11: Death, Sex, and Darshan 161

Chapter 12: The Hunt 177

Chapter 13: A Week of Headlessness 193

Chapter 14: No Flip Side to the Coin 203

Epilogue 219

Spiritual First Aid 225

Foreword

This book answers the question of how do you find the answer to who and what you are—ultimately—beyond any shadow of a doubt—beyond the body, and beyond the mind—both of which we all know in our heart, will perish… leaving what behind?

This book is not a philosophical treatise. Rather than presenting mere abstractions, this book tells of the actions that speak louder than words. Yet between the lines it conveys a profound philosophy and shows what it means to "walk the talk."

In this autobiographical telling of the story of his own spiritual path, Shawn Nevins engages us at a deeply and generously personal level, with candor and conviction, wit and wisdom, insight and inspiration. In the Epilogue, he shares how the successful conclusion of his search has impacted his life and leaves us with an optimistic message of encouragement. He ends the book with a distillation of the "take-aways" from his life, titled *Spiritual First Aid*, that offers wise and extremely valuable counsel to every spiritual seeker no matter what their practice or where they find themselves on the path right now.

Maybe you've heard of the author. He is far less well-known than he deserves to be.

Perhaps you've been exposed to his profound poetry, that is so reminiscent of Rumi, and evokes in the reader that very same sense of the Eternal in the present moment. Perhaps you've watched some of the remarkable video documentaries he has made of the spiritual search, and the journeys of those who have reached a conclusive end to it, and published under his *Poetry in Motion* imprimatur. Perhaps you've visited his web site SpiritualTeachers.org, one of the oldest and highest-ranked by search engines for that topic.

But if you've never heard of Shawn Nevins, his self-told story just might be the most valuable one you've heard in a very long time, because it just might be the one in which you can most easily see yourself.

And when you do, you might just become inspired to new depths of self-honesty and conviction that a spiritual path is worthwhile because finding those ultimate answers is indeed possible – when you search for them, as Nisargadatta says over and over in *I Am That* "in earnest" – and as Shawn's life's story so clearly represents.

Whatever else can be said about this book, it must be said loud and clear: This is what an authentic spiritual path looks like!

And for anyone who is familiar with the writings and recorded teachings of Richard Rose, founder of the TAT Foundation, mentor and teacher to countless seekers: This is what making a spiritual path your top priority looks like. This is what it looks like to become a reverse vector. This is what "retreat from untruth" looks like in one's life. This is what "living the life" looks like. This is what earnest self-inquiry looks like. This is what "going within" entails. This is how you transcend self-delusion and rationalization.

The book also reveals a bit of what it felt like to be in the presence of Richard Rose – and the conviction that he inspired in so many seekers that enlightenment was real—and a real possibility for you—If only you dedicated yourself to finding an answer, and if only you didn't postulate in advance what that answer had to be, and if only you were honest with yourself about what you in fact knew for sure—and didn't.

The value of group work, and what Rose called the *Law of the Ladder* and the *Contractor's Law*, is also illustrated in this book—again, not as a philosophical treatise, but revealed in the actions and consequences Shawn's story of his journey and work with fellow seekers makes apparent.

Given the enigmatic-sounding title, if you never heard of Shawn Nevins, or Richard Rose, or the TAT Foundation, I wonder what made you pick up this book to investigate if it is worth your time?

"Subtraction" seems an unlikely title to captivate your attention—even if you're a student of spirituality and/or psychology. After all, what does the single word convey?

Perhaps you intuited in the word "Subtraction" a hint that your life is basically one of addition and acquisition, and therein the suggestion of a solution to the futility of such for finding any ultimate meaning, or answers to the basic questions of birth, life and death: Who are you? What are you? Where did you come from (birth)? Where are you going (death)?

Such an intuition would mean the recognition exists somewhere deep within you that your own life has been a continuous process of adding psychological make-up and fancy clothes, and the acquisition of material things to define yourself to yourself—and to the world in which you must make your way.

Indeed, you've spent your whole life since birth, to this very moment, in an unbroken process of acquisition: building an identity in this world, acquiring knowledge, position, material possessions, a self you can believe in and feel good about—depositing the countless chits that you hope one day to cash in for earned spiritual rewards, however you conceive them.

Invariably those earned rewards involve some version of an immortal 'you' with no need for a body, to survive death, and while you live, some magnificently better version of you—better for having gained something that you previously did not possess.

Do you discover what you lack, or why such a feeling of dissatisfaction exists in the first place, by tasting new experiences? By learning new things? By "growth" practices that purportedly increase the size and scope of you? By expanding your consciousness? (Richard Rose once quipped that God himself would have to move out of the way to accommodate you and make room for your vast expansion.)

No. Discovery of that which IS—cannot be revealed by piling things on top of that which it is not—or by piling up a heap of things external to yourself, or painting a picture to look at, like some Rorschach image on which you will project the answer you want and need, instead of the objective Truth. It's the old cliché of man creating god in his image, yet we are so sure we are smarter than that, and so immune from what most others are not.

Subtraction of that which is not, is the universal path to the discovery of that which is. When everything false is removed, what is left must be true. Whatever you ultimately are, when everything about you that is not you has been subtracted, then what is left must be your true nature, the real essential, eternal you—that may not be a "you" at all…. If the body dies and is dissipated; If what we consider our precious possession of mind, is one with that very same body, and dies and is dissipated with that body; What can possibly remain of you?

A subtractive, deconstructive process is the surest way to successful conclusion of a spiritual path. It was the main piece of the shortcut that Richard Rose said existed. But just what in the world does subtraction on a spiritual path really mean? How could it translate into a viable spiritual practice? How does one follow a subtractive path?

That is precisely what this book is about, what it so eloquently reveals, and what it so satisfyingly illustrates, all in a way that frequently reminded me throughout my reading of it, that the author of these pages is also a talented and inspiring poet.

—Bob Cergol

The Prelude and the Purpose

To begin, is the hardest task there is;
to finish is the next hardest.

I appreciate writers who get to the point right away, then tell me a story to illustrate the point, then remind me again what the point was.

December 28, 1999 was the day my spiritual search ended. From late 1992 till that day, I devoted myself to finding an answer to the great philosophic questions of life: Who am I? What am I? What happens to me at death? These were not theological musings, but eminently practical questions that demanded answers based on personal experience rather than belief. I meditated for hundreds of hours, fasted, prayed, talked to spiritual teachers and talked to myself, spent days alone in the woods, tested and challenged my beliefs through dozens of practices, despaired and cried. A central theme of this path was that of a *Way of Subtraction* fueled by honesty. It was Richard Rose who taught me this simple, but elegant formula: "You back away from untruth," he said, turning from untruth until all that was left was what was real.

Just before the last day of the 20th century, my questions were put to rest. My notebook still contains the scribbling from that evening:

> God is here. He rings in the death of all we know.
> Rejoice, the end begins.
> A new life. Nothing ever the same. We are everlasting.
> Rejoice, I am free. Behind these words flows everlasting light.
> It is back there, doors open, look inside.
> This is my way, no plan, you cannot follow, but must try.
> God is here. God IS HERE Now.

I used the word God only as shorthand. "God" goes by many names. The Absolute, Buddha-Nature, Mind (with a capital "M"), Self (with a capital "S"), and the big "E" of Enlightenment. You have some conception in your mind the moment these words are read. That is unavoidable, but what happens next is not. You could be satisfied with the words, or you could ask what they really mean and seek that which inspired the words. This book is about the latter.

Enlightenment is just a word—a chew-toy for the mind. The desire in our heart for the truth is what we must connect with. That desire will guide us, but it is not easy to hear the heart and then take action. Such action is the work that leads to the backing away from untruth that is the spiritual path.

Why bother? Because a part of us longs for an answer to a question which is uniquely ours. I was asleep to that longing for many years. Embrace that longing. Allow it to grow. To follow a spiritual path is to follow that longing.

You do not realize the depth of your uncertainty. Nor can you conceive what it means to know one thing for certain, and how that makes all the difference in the world. My hope is this story, which is unique to me, will inspire you to continue your path.

Chapter 1:
End of Life One

Everyone has two lives.
The second one begins when you realize you only have one.

— *Steven Sotloff*

"Who am I?" would have been a meaningless question to the young man that was me, alone on the first Saturday evening of freshman year at the University of Kentucky. Eighteen years old, oblivious to the force of motives, I was ruled by fears and desires that seemed my own. There was no separation between the thoughts and feelings that flared through the mind, and my awareness of them. I was, as a friend expressed years later, completely laminated to whatever I experienced. There was only the reaching ache of loneliness and the silent complaint, "Why me?"

Fear led me to this isolation. Rather than knocking on a neighbor's door and introducing myself, or saying hi in the hallway, I felt the presence of strangers like a pointed accusation. Avoiding the anxiety, I pretended: I am busy, I am important, I am special. I walked hurriedly from place to place with an imagined air of self-importance. I rehearsed conversations that entranced audiences who never appeared. It was a hellish circular prison where I wanted to hide the fact I was alone, yet did not want to be alone. This pretending gave a feeling of control, as if directing my little boat of self through life—though in reality it lacked compass, engine, or even steering wheel. I was not aware enough to wonder why I hid while others leapt into new encounters, or to question my control of the collection of thoughts and feelings called "Shawn."

Though fear and uncertainty predominated, there was a deeply buried longing. I didn't acknowledge it, but my body and mind savored the outdoors. The summer before freshman year, I reviewed the University's course catalog, starting at the letter "A": accounting, agriculture, arts, biology, chemistry, engineering, mathematics and so on. In the agriculture section, I lingered on photos of the light dappled, rolling green hills of Kentucky horse country. In the mind's eye, an image unfolded of a wide field under a clear, azure sky. Sun-warmed air rose from the grass, surrounding me in a feeling of contentment. It was a perfect moment that was mine to have if I could find that place. I would someday stand under that azure sky, and everything would be perfect. Though I had never milked a cow, ridden a tractor, or even grown a vegetable, these photos drew me to agriculture, and I settled on it as my career. I told no one of this dream, especially not my advisor at the agriculture school. I doubt he could have corrected my misunderstanding—that happiness was created by circumstances we create. Instead, I plunged headlong into a science-heavy schedule of classes, chasing the dream that a career would lead me to that place of complete satisfaction.

I was far from any sort of satisfaction that first weekend of school. Fleeing the image of myself as a loser sitting alone in the dormitory, I wound up sitting alone on a park bench behind the student center. There, I briefly held the hope I looked like a brooding loner—too cool to bother with parties and friends. But that was not where or who I wanted to be. I longed to laugh, to meet girls, and impress the world with my personality. Instead, I churned on every flaw: I saw myself as shy, stupid, ugly, weak, scared, skinny…

Suddenly my thoughts flipped from their miserable litany, and a moment of grace entered. The green pine boughs swaying high overhead caught my attention as if whispering my name. The mind quieted, and in that space I felt the wind push at my hair, and heard the soft rustle of pine needles brushing one another. No longer was I drowning in thought. The silence built, thickening as if a storm was coming, but all was quiet and at peace, inside and out. Something *other than me* was present—not alien, but familiar and comforting, as if I were again a child in the back seat of my parent's car, safely drifting to sleep under the muffled sound of their voices. I doubt this feeling lasted a minute, but the loneliness and anxiety were gone.

I had no context for this strange event—as any notion of spirituality was utterly absent from my world view. Nor was there any thought that I should seek out the cause of this state, or that others might have experienced something similar. Nor was there recognition that the instant relief of my troubles occurred without any change in my outer circumstances. I could be alone without feeling lonely. How was this possible? I would never know because I couldn't even ask the question. In the coming days, it became apparent that I was not freed from the weight of fear, but my self-criticism and dissatisfaction receded as chemistry class and calculus presented more immediate concerns.

The routine of class and homework comfortably consumed my life. I sat in the same seat each day, rarely speaking to classmates because I couldn't compose the perfect opening line. Throwing my energy into schoolwork solved the boredom and unease of my first freshman weeks. Through brute force memorization, reading and re-reading my notes and textbooks, I rose almost, but not quite to the top of my classes.

Relationships became road signs passed on the way elsewhere. I told myself I was in school to get good grades rather than make friends. The only connection I admitted to wanting was with a girlfriend, and the courage finally arose to introduce myself to the cute blonde seated next to me on a field trip. The initial thrill of getting her phone number became a crushing defeat when I called the next weekend, and her roommate said Megan was washing her hair. I left my phone number, but she never called back. After our next class, we awkwardly stood in the hall as Megan told me about her boyfriend. I remember she looked away a lot while we talked. Words I didn't want to hear fragmented and lodged in my memory. I still thought she was beautiful. I smiled and pretended not to care, but never spoke to her again. Phrases festered in my mind: "I'm an idiot. Not good looking, not cool, and a fool."

I went home to my parents for the summer after a mostly forgettable freshman year. Though a high school dropout, my dad had a wide-ranging curiosity with a library to match. There were books on the Old West and World War II, detective novels and adventure stories, and authors like Mark Twain, Edgar Allen Poe, and Harlan Hubbard. Browsing the collection, I came upon *Arnold: The Education of a Bodybuilder*. There was the story of Arnold Schwarzenegger's rise from sickly child to champion bodybuilder. While I dabbled in my dad's garage gym throughout high school, I lacked the needed motivation. Now however, being "awesome and powerful" as Arnold put it, was exactly what I wanted. Rather than asking out more girls, I would first make myself into a real man, so awesome and powerful, that I would never again feel the sting of rejection.

I threw myself into lifting weights, and was ecstatic to learn my new dorm for the sophomore year had a gym. Its windowless basement harbored a collection of well-worn exercise equipment that I attended to with religious devotion an hour each day. Between lifting weights and frequenting the all-you-can-eat dining hall, I slowly armored myself with muscle over the course of the year. Not fully content with my transformation, I grew my hair long, and adopted a facade of ripped jeans, flannel shirts, and chains which I copied from a lab partner whom I was certain was cool. Yet Frank, a droopy, ever-present, and thickly bearded fixture on the front porch of our dorm, was not impressed. From beneath the brim of his filthy baseball cap, he called out "Hey, ya big stiff!" every time he saw me. I couldn't even fool the most unhip guy in the dorm, much less attract any ladies. At least not yet. If I added more muscle and more hip clothing, surely things would change.

Nothing did. After months of this crafted persona, I felt a lurking dissatisfaction with my non-existent social life, occasionally depressing me enough to ask "What's the point?" Which is a form of one of the oldest philosophical questions: What is the purpose of life? Was there any purpose to the misery I experienced? Because if not, a fleeting but familiar voice said, maybe I should end it all now. A week finally arrived where I could no longer ignore this question, and I went to the only place I knew to seek answers—the library. In the cool, hushed recesses of its stacks, I bypassed the religion section and picked a book of Zen poetry from the Eastern philosophy shelf. I have no idea why I thought Zen could answer my question, but I did think this exotic book would impress anyone who saw me reading it. Though it looked nice on my desk, I puzzled over the poems and found nothing intelligible:

Fathomed at last!
Ocean's dried. Void burst.
Without an obstacle in sight,
It's everywhere!

This was a bunch of riddles rather than an answer to life's purpose. Casting aside my short study of Zen, the black and white of science made more sense, and I concluded that life was simply biological. Everything died, and a higher purpose was not necessary to live and enjoy life. For a time, this conclusion put the metaphysical questions to rest. I was helped, (or hindered I would later decide) by the stubborn regularity of my routines of study and exercise, even the same paths I walked each day to class gave me a bit of comfort. Habit carried me through any sloughs of depression. Plus, I still had the dream that my best years were yet to come.

I once complained to a teacher in high school that, "These are supposed to be the best years of my life," but it certainly didn't feel that way.

"Oh no," she said, "college will be the best. You'll love college."

Now that I was in college, I hoped like hell these were not the best years. It must be graduate school, I thought, or maybe even after I graduated when I got a house and a wife and all the possessions that led to a happy life.

By my junior year, despite my fear of people and telling myself they were unnecessary, I recognized the need to interact. A professor recommended joining the agronomy club, as this would look good on my graduate school applications. With only four members, it wasn't long before I wound up president. Surprisingly, I enjoyed arranging pizza parties and service projects that grew the club from four to eight members. Having a clear role to play in a small group helped me understand how to interact. Another professor suggested a prestigious internship at Argonne National Laboratory, so I spent the summer there. My senior year, the recommendation was for independent research, so I prepared a presentation for a conference in California. I was on a train where people kept handing out tickets for further stops. You want to give me a ticket to graduate school? Sure, why not?

My junior and senior years were not all work. The Block and Bridle Club was famous for its alcohol-fueled barn parties, and I drunkenly fell into more than one stack of hay bales, though never with a girl in hand. In those short, blurry moments it did not matter how much muscle I had or whether I had something witty to say. I could see acceptance in the eyes of others—I was fun to be around—

and for that night at least I was "normal." Inebriation was the only state which lessened my fear, as the rest of the time I was ever the anxious actor perpetually waiting in the wings practicing his lines.

Not until the last weeks of my senior year did I relax my routines, as I realized that no graduate school would see my final grades. I skipped classes to go for a drive. I took a hike with a girl I liked and even made time to sit with Frank on the front porch. I suddenly wished for time to slow. On the last day of school, I looked down the now quiet and empty length of our hall and realized I missed an opportunity. I wanted to reach out, but there was no one left to receive my hand. My one wish was that I had spent more time socializing and enjoying myself.

The next stop, however, was a Master's Degree at North Carolina State University's soil science department. Looking for a fresh start to my social life, I was disappointed by the cold and unwelcoming brick façade of NCSU's graduate student housing. No one left their doors open or chatted in the hallway, and there was no front porch. My major professor, who would mentor me for the next two years, proved a dour sort as well. Our first meeting lasted five minutes, then his assistant showed me to my office.

As a graduate student, I was granted a desk in the corner of a third-floor laboratory. There amongst the fume hoods, test tubes and deionized water, I claimed a space—arranging my text books on a shelf like trophies. I propped my boots on the smooth black surface of the lab bench, then looked out the window at the brick courtyard filled with students moving between classes. Briefly, I felt like the king of the world.

Classes were hard, however, and disappointments revealed themselves one after another. I struggled to stay awake in class as an unusual fatigue wove itself into my days. I didn't appreciate my Indian roommate whose cooking spices permeated our room. I missed my family. I learned that research was often guided more by funding fads than any great desire for scientific exploration. Even the red clay topsoil of North Carolina was dry and hard compared to the dark, rich, and crumbly central Kentucky loam. "Why did I even want to go to grad school?" I wondered. Looking for friends, I forced myself to attend a graduate student association party one evening, and there I met Ann.

"Why can't I know the joy of love? Why must I be me?" With such a journal entry within a few days of meeting Ann, it was no surprise this ended badly. Though too timid to ask her phone number that evening, I regained my courage the next day and knocked on every lab door in her department until I found her.

For the first time in my shy life, I pursued a girl—as in flirted, pestered, and generally, genially stalked her until the weight of my attention turned her mind to me. She smiled when I talked with her as if I mattered, and that sense of belonging drew me like the grass on that long sought Kentucky hillside. That she had a boyfriend in another state meant nothing to me. With enough persistence and effort, I opened a crack in the world of possibilities and jumped in with abandon. A short month of uncertainty, feverish thoughts, longing, heartache, and occasional joy followed. In the midst of it, I wrote in my journal, "I've noticed that I'm not a very happy person." Then, though she was never wholly mine, Ann ended our brief romance. It felt like the one light, the one hope and dream of my life was gone.

The wreckage was total—disillusionment with graduate school, and the loss of the woman I managed to entangle in my equation for happiness. Ann said she wanted to be friends, and I sat on the front stoop of her apartment crying into her shoulder, desperately hiding from an overwhelming blackness that rose up in my mind and threatened to swallow me. I was suddenly and mysteriously terrified by the thought of forever being alone. This was far deeper than any loneliness I previously experienced. This was a cold, dark universe staring at the inconsequential speck that was me.

Days passed like a long, heaving sigh until late October, when I saw a poster advertising a lecture. "What is Enlightenment?" it said, and I wondered if therein lay an answer to my troubles. My imagined life with Ann seemed full of purpose, but now I found no reason to live. I felt weak, with no energy for exercise and little motivation for class. My self-proclaimed conclusion of biological mortality offered no comfort. Instead, it shouted my stark meaninglessness to a silent universe.

Tuesday evening, I slid into a crowded lecture hall, and found a place near the back. The lecturer was Richard Rose. A short, stocky man, nearly bald, with a wispy white goatee, he wore a non-descript sport coat and collared shirt with no tie. He seemed at ease on the podium, though slightly disorganized, laughing as he rummaged through his pockets looking for reading glasses. He sifted through an old vinyl portfolio, and pulled forth a sheaf of papers. He began to read:

"Does a man own a house, or does the house own him?"
"Does a man have power, or is he overpow-ered?"
"Does a man enjoy or is he consumed?"
"Can a man become?"
"How shall he know what he should become?"

The lecture continued like this for over an hour. My mind went quiet under a stream of questions for which I had no answers. Rose's eyes scanned the room and, now and then, it felt he looked directly at me and spoke to me alone. Telling me, "This is important." This feeling was uncanny and weighty. I recognized Rose had *something*, and I wanted to know more. After the lecture, I put my name on a mailing list for the group that sponsored this lecture: the Self Knowledge Symposium. The mind is ever forgetful, though, so I was surprised when a few days later a fellow named Bill called to invite me to a meeting. That meeting would mark the end of life one, and the beginning of a nine-year spiritual path best described as a *Way of Subtraction*.

Chapter 2:
What Shall You Become?

*Does man fall in love with anything
besides his own self and his projections?*

—*Richard Rose*

The Self Knowledge Symposium (SKS) met in Harrelson Hall, which had the lowly distinction of being the only round building on campus and was historically regarded as "one of the most unsatisfactory academic buildings imaginable." Everything was pie-shaped: classrooms, offices, even the bathrooms. Unmarked exterior doors conspired with a spiral ramp which circled the outside of the building, to leave students perpetually unsure as to which floor they were on, or which direction to go to reach a classroom. I half-suspect the SKS met there because whoever doled out room assignments viewed this as fitting punishment for what was surely a cult.

Whatever misgivings I had about the architecture did not carry over to the group itself. That first meeting was a revelation courtesy of a middle-aged businessman named August Turak. Though ostensibly a student group, "Augie" ran the show. Augie introduced Richard Rose at the prior week's lecture, where he struck me as remarkably stiff and ill at ease. Not so at the SKS. Sipping a two-liter of caffeinated Diet Coke, his eyes sparkled as he effortlessly held the attention of everyone in the room.

"This is you," he said, bending his six foot, two hundred pound frame to draw a straight line low on the chalkboard.

"You live on this line, between the poles of opposites: black and white, good and bad, pleasure and pain." Exactly, I thought. I was tired of being on the painful side, but I recognized that bouncing between the poles was the summary of my life.

"Where you want to be is up here," he said, smacking a chalk mark above the line. "Up here, you look down upon the opposites and see they aren't opposites at all. They are gradations on a line. You'll never know that as long as you're living on the line." That transcendence, looking down on the opposites, was immediately appealing, though I had never encountered the idea.

Augie's voice thrust forward, radiating confidence and conviction. When someone asked a question, he paused, eyes riveted and mouth slightly open as if taking in their every word, then peered behind the question to address its motivation, or launched a question in reply. I was not prepared to engage in this swordplay. Towards the end of the evening, he boldly stroked the formula for success across the chalkboard: Right Thinking + Right Action + Time = Results. I furiously recorded his words in my notebook, as if my life depended on it, which it probably did.

The radical shift catalyzed by the SKS appeared like a bright line in my journal. November 1st was a typical, depressing post-Ann day, as I wrote, "This last week was the most miserable of my life…" By November 13th, however, I waxed philosophical:

The world is a movie; the projector is God… Plato's man chained in a cave… he thought shadows were reality and did not know to turn around and look to the light… I am guilty of trying to give meaning to my life by loving someone else. This is not the way. I am guilty of trying to give meaning to my life through work. This is not the way.

While Richard Rose's talk impressed me with an inkling of the profound, it was Augie's talk that provided insights immediately applicable to my current misery. The sad fact was that nothing in my upbringing or years in school had provided tools for understanding my psychology. Before that first SKS meeting, I never considered objectively looking at why I did the things I did. Self-knowledge and self-study were utterly new to me. Over the next couple of months, I did not miss a meeting.

Though he seemed big, brash, and ballsy, Augie rarely talked about himself. In time, I learned that he worked at MTV in its heady early days, was a protégé of IBM's legendary Louis Mobley, worked as a salesman and consultant and stockpiled money along the way. One of the first students of Richard Rose from the 1970s, Augie kept a core of philosophic discontent through all his worldly adventures and his off-and-on relationship with Rose. He founded the SKS as a platform for introducing students to a practical philosophy of life and, in particular, to the teachings of Rose.

Each week, ten or twelve students gathered for an hour and a half meeting—most in their early twenties, predominately guys and a surprising number of engineering/math/computer science types. I expected a room dominated by philosophy and psychology students, but by all appearances they seemed uninterested in the ad hoc approach to self-study that the SKS provided.

Augie thrilled our impressionable minds with stories often culled from the *Wall Street Journal* or his wide network of connections. He was a masterful storyteller who loved tales of people summoning their determination to accomplish the extraordinary.

Augie espoused a warrior/monk/entrepreneur hybrid—equal parts Arthurian knight, Zen master, and start-up CEO. This superman was noble, brave, focused, concentrated, intense, and pure of intent. The kind of person who set goals and achieved them; not wasting time, but approaching life as if their hair was on fire. Whatever Jesus had in mind when he said the meek shall inherit the Earth, Augie was not interested. Augie was not the kind to use words like "maybe," "possibly," and "perhaps." He favored the obsessed and driven, turning an article on a Scrabble champion into an example of single-minded devotion leading to success.

Augie frequently used the word "Zen" in the context of his stories. Like Richard Rose, Augie saw Zen as a system of tension rather than a serene exercise in meditation and withdrawal from the world. Keep your head on a problem until it, or you, cracked—then an answer was revealed.

"Attention means 'at tension!'" Augie said, driving home the word "tension" like a spike. Many Zen Buddhists would have been dismayed by this appropriation of Zen. However, in extracting the components of discipline and concentration applied to an intractable problem, Rose and Augie both felt they stripped away accumulated centuries of Zen barnacles and revealed the solid essence of the practice. Add to that, Zen sounded cool to a bunch of college kids.

The SKS had a recommended book list, and being ever the good student I started checking off the titles. While it would be some years before I realized the futility of looking to books for a solution to existential questions, at this early stage books were an invaluable in training the mind to question its assumptions. Within the first few pages of P.D. Ouspensky's *The Psychology of Man's Possible Evolution*, a circular diagram called "The General Picture of Man" riveted my attention. The circle was divided into tiny blocks labeled "I."

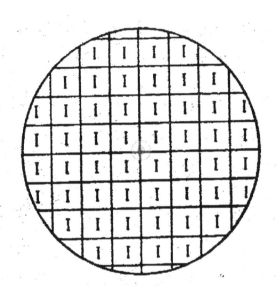

"In reality, there is no oneness in man and there is no controlling center, no permanent 'I' or ego," said Ouspensky.

"Each of these 'I's' represents at every given moment a very small part of our 'brain,' 'mind,' or 'intelligence,' but each of them means itself to represent *the whole*. When man says 'I' it sounds as if he meant the whole of himself, but really even when he himself thinks that he means it, it is only a passing thought, a passing mood, or passing desire."

I nodded in agreement as I turned the pages. What Ouspensky described, I saw in my behavior though I never considered why. Before that day, if you asked me who I was I would have simply said "me." Now however, that certainty wavered as I saw the collection of often competing desires that masqueraded as a unified whole.

"Man must know what he has and what he has not," Ouspensky said. It was clear I knew neither.

For the first time in my life, rather than believing I was each desire that appeared in my mind, I stood back and noticed some of them were cranky visitors. In doing so, I took a small step up from the line of opposites Augie described. Who am I? I am Shawn. I am a grad student, a cool guy, invincible, doomed, a friend, a failure, a human being. This list went on and on like the expanse of "I's" in Ouspensky's diagram.

Some of these "I's" were not just passing fancies, however. A select core were long-standing, cherished beliefs that dominated my view of the world. I moved through life like a meaning-seeking machine in a land of cardboard cutouts. I projected love upon a cutout called "girlfriend." A cutout called "career" provided status, and a cutout called "home" provided security and peace. These additions were tangible evidence of the meaning of my life. Furthermore, if I got the career, home, and girl-friend cutouts aligned just so, then I would be content—at last fully alive. I was so certain of the circumstances of this imagined state, that I conceived it in great detail: Sitting on the front porch swing of a white wood farmhouse. The weather t-shirt perfect, without a mosquito or fly in sight. Swaying back and forth, a slight breeze soothing my skin. My gaze drifting across the lawn and into the mingled branches of an expanse of trees. Inside, the clink of a spoon on glass as my wife prepared lemonade. Every need suspended, the world balanced in quiet satisfaction. Augie described it as the sigh of relief that you finally "made it."

Despite my identification of these dream components, the feeling of a future perfect moment still compelled me. It was the same feeling of contentment that arose when I saw photos of Kentucky horse country and latched onto a career in agriculture as the path to that place. What finally shook my faith in the dream was the first time I heard Augie's piercing observation: The moment of perfection does not last, and the thought "now what?" inevitably follows. I had never considered that the stars of my perfect moment would align for minutes if not seconds, then continue their course. The character on the swing had to get up, go to work, mow the lawn, answer the phone, and drain the last drop from his lemonade. The perfect moment fell into the past, submerged by the mind's ever insistent question: "And now what?" It was as if the human machine was programmed for dissatisfaction and restlessness.

As my mind opened to questioning my beliefs, other possibilities arose. Augie spun the enticing tale of a mystical state called enlightenment. Enlightenment was not a swan dive into bliss, but a cataclysmic revelation of one's true nature brought about by extreme tension, focus, and desire. While Augie had worldly achievement, it was Rose who had enlightenment.

While I had no clue what enlightenment really meant, I wanted to know more. Augie used to say "You've got to fatten up the head before you chop it off." The "chop it off" referred to enlightenment. It was somehow good to have your head metaphorically chopped off…
I bought a copy of Rose's *The Albigen Papers*, hoping the enlightened master would tell why this was a good thing. Instead, I got more questions and an understanding that there was a path, however vague, to spiritual realization. Part of that path was to "fatten up the head," which as it turned out was much of what the SKS provided. To fatten up the head meant absorbing knowledge through books and meetings, and the paradoxical exercise of strengthen-ing character through questioning beliefs. As assumptions and false beliefs were revealed, then from the many false I's in Ouspensky's drawing, I progressed towards the true one. This process only happened through intense work. In Rose's case, finding the true self was actually a tran-scendence of self that he equated with death of the ego. Not only was your head chopped off, but you died… and still this was a good thing. I didn't know enough yet to be scared of the possibility.

A small group of us began to apply Augie's advice to our daily life rather than just listen to his Thursday night stories. Our motivations were mixed at best. I wanted relief from misery, others saw enlightenment as an intellectual puzzle, others saw it as a great adventure, and some just liked being a part of an unusual group. No one wanted their head cut off, but it didn't matter at that point what inspired us to action. All that mattered was to begin.

Augie was an advocate of action. "Just hit something," was a favorite saying of his. He'd tell the story of youth football coaches dismayed to see their tiny, uncertain players standing on the field amidst the action. "Just hit something," they would yell. Just hitting something was better than standing still. Taking the risk and exercising force brought wisdom.

In the context of the SKS, action took many forms. For me, it meant struggling to speak up during meetings, ask questions, and allow my beliefs to be tested. Action meant engaging with life rather than just observing. It was not easy for an introvert, and no easier now than my awkward social attempts as an undergrad.

But I was motivated. I also started testing my ability to accomplish tasks and keep commitments. I challenged *my self* to not always retreat from the uncomfortable. I began to think of myself as my *self*—and this is key—a separate self with behaviors and patterns to study. I undertook numerous character-building challenges. Afraid of the dark, I stayed late into the night at one of the University's research farms. Afraid of public speaking, I read one of Richard Rose's poems—with voice quavering and knees shaking—at an open mic night in a local bar. I fasted, gave up sweets and spicy foods, and noted in a journal my reactions and thoughts about these experiments, especially how I tried to talk my self out of doing them. Not every undertaking was a success. Hearing of spiritual seekers who spend days on retreat, I took a blanket into the woods and committed to sitting there the entire day with nothing to distract me. I left after three hours as bugs landed on me, the sun chased away the shade, my back hurt, and one minute seemed multiplied by five. I belatedly realized sitting without a plan of what to focus on led to a bored brain looking for any excuse to leave.

The motivations behind my actions came under deep scrutiny. For some weeks, I obsessively mulled over buying an equalizer and pre-amp for my stereo system. Why did that thought keep popping into my mind? I dug into memories to see where the desire originated, but what ultimately proved more useful was imagining already owning the gear. It dawned on me that more than improving my music listening experience, what I really desired was to impress people with my discerning tastes. My ego, my sense of being an individual in this world, was strengthened through acquisition—even if all I did was imagine how others appreciated the new me. Not only that, but the entire consumer culture was built on providing ever more exotic and expensive products to feed the ego. No matter how good my stereo became, it could always be better, and a nagging incompleteness shadowed each purchase.

Even my music collection, carefully chosen to appear eclectic and hip, was symptomatic of a never-ending quest to create an identity that won admiration. Acting on this realization, I gave away the stereo and albums, and felt surprisingly at ease rather than regretful. I cut my long hair and put away the necklaces, ripped jeans and other symbols that helped me feel cool and unique despite the slights of the world. These subtractive actions brought relief, like a bodybuilder relaxing after holding a pose too long. Looking back, I wondered how much Frank's "big stiff" greetings stemmed from him seeing poses I could not.

This subtraction was the beginning of backing away from untruth—Rose's path to ultimate Truth (i.e. enlightenment). Backing away, what he called the Law of the Reversed Vector, was one step on the path that I grasped from *The Albigen Papers*:

> The Law of the Reversed Vector states that you cannot approach the Truth. You must become (a vector), but you cannot *learn* the absolute Truth. Not knowing the Truth in the beginning, nor even the true path, we still wish to move toward the Truth. We find that there is only one way, and that is to first build of ourselves a very determined person, – a vector. We cut off tangential dissipaters of energy and ball up this energy for the work ahead. And then like most

of the clergy, we make the mistake of putting years of this precious energy into first one blind direction and then another… until we learn that we must reverse the vector.

We must back into the Truth by backing away from untruth.

There was a lot packed into that paragraph. I could not learn the truth—it was not knowledge to be acquired. Cutting out distractions brought focus. Identify what was obviously not true, like my Arnold Schwarzenegger-inspired delusions of awesomeness, and abandon it.

Within three extraordinary months of attending Rose's lecture, I wrote, "…the SKS is as important as school." As other students came and went, I stuck around and became a core member. With no girlfriend and no friends outside of the SKS, it was easy to regularly attend meetings and devote time to sustaining the group. I walked the campus with posters under my arm and a stapler in hand, covering bulletin boards and kiosks with advertisements for our group. It was a point of pride to hang more posters than anyone else.

While the Thursday night meetings were for students only, there was another meeting at Augie's house. As soon as I heard about it, I asked if I could go. About half the attendees were in their thirties or forties, while the rest were students or recent graduates. As an invitation-only group, the members were more consistent in attendance and consequently more open and familiar with one another. For the first time, I witnessed in-depth "confrontation"—one of the practices of Rose's system.

Augie's sparsely furnished condominium had just enough couches and kitchen chairs to keep us from spilling onto the floor. There was a palpable feel of excitement as he introduced a line from *Apocalypse Now* for the evening's topic: "You have to have men who are moral... and at the same time who are able to utilize their primordial instincts to kill without feeling... without passion... without judgment... without judgment! Because it's judgment that defeats us." Augie then opened the floor to discussion. Opinions flew back and forth while Augie listened, waiting for an angle of attack. Someone's opinion made a subtle shift from logical discussion to a thought tinged with emotion, as the mind contracted and defensively took a position behind a barricade of belief. Augie pounced, probing and questions, as the meeting pivoted from the conceptual to the personal.

I was in awe of the process, but afraid to participate. At its best, confrontation was a Socratic dialogue in which Augie challenged a participant's beliefs. It was similar to the self-questioning I engaged in, but amplified and accelerated. Augie was extremely skilled at getting to the root of assumptions, though not immune to his personal beliefs colliding with those of another. At that point, the joint exploration of dialogue descended into argument. Most nights I sat silently unless Augie invited me in with

"So Shawn, what do you think?" That was as rare as a lack of opinions.

My reticence was an impediment in confrontation, but I pushed forward in other ways. Four of us rented an old bungalow in the Boylan Heights neighborhood of Raleigh and dubbed it the "Zen Den." There was Eric, a tall, square-jawed adventurer, engineer and lover of languages; Doug, even taller, a frenetic musician and physics grad student; and Danny, a gifted raconteur with the haunted eyes of someone who had taken a bad drug trip or two. We attempted to channel our energies more and more onto the spiritual path by surrounding ourselves with like-minded seekers. Rather than talking about sports, it was the sort of place where your roommate read philosophy at the breakfast table. We meditated together on Sunday mornings. A copy of *The Zen Teaching of Huang Po* sat in the bathroom. For a Friday night party, we invited other SKS members over to watch *Henry V*. In the film, Kenneth Branagh's St. Crispen's Day speech captured the feeling of our little home: "We few, we happy few, we band of brothers."

If all this seems cult-like, it was. Yet it was a good-natured cult. The SKS challenged people to become more competent, honest, and trustworthy. People rose to the challenge. A few took those skills and applied them to the spiritual search, while others simply became better human beings.

The SKS was a crucible, accelerating insights that normally required many years and it reflected Mr. Rose's statement that, "I'm looking to age a few young people." In a miraculous few months, I learned that much of what I thought true was belief rather than wisdom culled from experience. Seventeen years of education had only piled belief upon belief.

My wayward drift from my graduate school dreams was spotlighted by the exit seminar of a retiring professor. Gray-bearded and bespectacled, he began with a story:

"I was a young graduate student in Honduras, spending the summer on a research farm. I lived in what was just a hut, really, with a lantern as my only light. A few days in, I sat down after a long day in the field and looked over the books on the shelf above my bed."

His long pause captured my attention.

"There on the shelf is a thin, faded volume. It is the book that will change my life."

I was on the edge of my seat in anticipation.

"It was a study of strip cropping in tropical ecosystems."

As if someone slapped me awake from a deep sleep, I looked around the room and realized I was in a land of sleepwalkers.

The next evening, my happiness in sitting amongst spiritual comrades was clear. Augie started the meeting with this Theodore Roosevelt quote:

The credit belongs to the man who is actually in the arena, whose face is marred by dust and sweat and blood, who strives valiantly, who errs and comes up short again and again, who knows the great enthusiasms, the great devotions, and spends himself in a worthy cause…

"What is your worthy cause to be?" was Augie's question to us.

I did not know the answer to that, but I did at last know happiness among friends.

Chapter 3:
The Haunting Presence
of Richard Rose

Rose said we were still concerned with what we might miss if
we chose a spiritual path. We had no conception of what was at
stake and what there was to gain from seeking.

I wasn't ready to declare my worthy cause as enlightenment. For one, I had no idea what it really meant,
and two, I was both attracted to and wary of the spiritual
search. Years later, I recognized this mix of attraction and
fear in the words of the Zen Patriarch Huang Po:

> The substance of the Absolute is inwardly like
> wood or stone, in that it is motionless, and out-
> wardly like the void, in that it is without bounds
> or obstructions… Those who hasten toward it
> dare not enter, fearing to hurtle down through

the void with nothing to cling to or to stay their fall. So they look to the brink and retreat.[1]

I would encounter that brink many times and in many forms during the coming years. For now though, I only recognized that a spiritual path demanded change and that change involved abandoning old behaviors. It was one thing to improve my character and abandon pretenses, but another entirely to pursue enlightenment. Eric felt enlightenment was the ultimate adventure, but I wasn't so sure, nor was I sure there was even such a thing as enlightenment. Maybe Richard Rose was just crazy.

On a cold and overcast March weekend, I and a dozen other SKS members squeezed into a rental van and made a pilgrimage to Rose's home. "The Farm" was a nine-hour journey north of Raleigh, across the sweep of the weathered Appalachians. Leaving the interstate, the dreary neighborhood of Elm Grove was our gateway to another world. A shallow, roadside creek wound further and further into a worn-out countryside. The atmosphere was dipped in gray, making the people, buildings, roads, even the sky, look decades past their prime. Turning off the paved road, we bounced and climbed higher and higher up a rutted gravel lane. The ground to the left of the lane fell off so abruptly that we peered into the tops of enormous maples and oaks. In the midst of modern-day

---

1   *The Zen Teaching of Huang Po,* translated by John Blofeld, Shambhala, 1994.

America, it felt like the end of the earth, as if we would travel the final miles on foot and navigate by the stars. Thankfully, the lane leveled out, dipped, then revealed Rose's weathered white-board farmhouse standing behind a fort-like wooden fence. We pulled into his yard, directly in front of a faded green outhouse with the word "Men" scrawled across the door. The ground was mushy and uneven, as if it too was weary of holding a pretense of solidity.

To the side of Rose's farmhouse, a meeting room jutted out on stilts like a tacked-on afterthought. Crossing its threshold, a wall of heat fogged my glasses. Mr. Rose greeted us one by one, his eyes squinted from smiling as he shook our hands. His grip seemed relaxed, but when I squeezed a bit harder, there was iron underneath. I grabbed a chair and assessed the surroundings as my glasses cleared. The walls, ceiling, and floor were rough, painted wood. Along the edge of the room, repurposed green and brown bus seats served as chairs. The only windows were high on the walls, just small slits like in a basement. The room smelled of old vinyl, dust, wood smoke and chicken soup—a slurry mixed by the heat from a fifty-five gallon drum that served as the wood stove. Rose tossed in another log and a blast of smoke poured into the room.

Mr. Rose's wife, Cecy, stepped in to say hi. She was tall and thin, with long dark hair and tired eyes. She spent most of the time in the kitchen, laboring to produce the

sandwiches and soup sold at a little counter on the side
of the room. In this unpretentious atmosphere we settled
down with our food while Rose, fueled by little more than
coffee and pie, talked and answered questions into the late
night. He seemed willing to devote as much time from his
life as we were willing to spend from ours. It was a quality
I came to admire deeply.

Both Augie and Rose had remarkable, sparkling
eyes. While Augie's eyes would go wide as if taking in and
evaluating all you said, Rose's eyes would narrow as if
drilling into some part of you that you didn't even know
existed. Much of the time, though, Rose seemed like an
ordinary man with a gift for storytelling. He regaled us
with fantastical tales of the hillbillies, farmers, crooked
judges and cops, and other characters that inhabited the
run-down, former steel-producing valley of Wheeling,
West Virginia. He seemed capable of telling such stories
all day, if not for our questions prompting a turn to
spiritual matters. He pivoted easily to his life-long pursuit
of philosophy: enrolling in a Catholic seminary as a
young boy, pursuing spiritualist phenomena, practicing
yoga, traveling the country looking for esoteric groups
and reading a good percentage of nearly every spiritual
teaching he could get his hands on in the 1930s through
1940s. After years of seeking, his enlightenment occurred
in 1947. He referred to it as a death experience, as all he
held to be his "self" was ripped away—his ego died—and
revealed in its absence was an indescribable state: the

Absolute. An inspired writing titled "Three Books of the Absolute" came to him in the weeks after this event. This poetic account of an ultimately impossible to conceive state ended with the words "All that remains is All." This revelation of the Absolute was enlightenment.

Afterwards, Rose married and raised three children. There was little time for more than dabbling in spiritual interests with a few half-hearted associates. He kept his family farm and thrifty, Depression-era ways, while making a living painting houses. When the 1960s brought a revolution and spiritual awakening among the young people in this country, Mr. Rose seized this open door and offered his farm as a refuge for seekers of truth. Though Rose did not find any serious students among the hippies that constituted this first wave, he kept meeting interested people. One of these was Keith Ham, to whom Rose leased property that, much to Rose's chagrin, became a large and scandal-mired Hare Krishna community. By the early 1970s, Rose was lecturing on college campuses and published *The Albigen Papers*. This book was his message in a bottle—at once a scathing critique of the hypocrisies and assumptions of American society, and an outline of the search for spiritual truth. Before long, a small ashram formed around him at his West Virginia farm and called itself the TAT (Truth and Transmission) Society.

Far from a love and light guru, Rose's confrontational style never attracted the crowds like Maharishi Mahesh Yogi, Alan Watts, or Ram Das. Ironically, while hundreds gathered at the Hare Krishna temple next to his property, TAT membership was never much over one hundred. An iconoclast at heart, Rose felt an affinity with the early Zen masters such as Hui Neng and Huang Po, and Rose's students often spoke of him as a Zen master though he had no lineage, no robe or bowl and saw most contemporary Zen as mired in tradition.

For Rose, Zen was a system of tension where the false faces of personality, and the judgments we made and displayed about ourselves, were transcended through questioning. Traditional Zen koans such as "Does the dog have a Buddha-nature?" were a method of applying tension through questions. Rose's questions, as epitomized in the "Lecture of Questions" I attended in Raleigh, were more direct: Does a person seduce another, or are both seduced? Do we think or imagine we think? What do you know for sure? Each of these questions was fundamentally as puzzling as the Buddha-nature of a dog.

Rather than meditation, Rose's first advice was to "get your house in order" and become capable of setting and reaching goals. To a large extent, this is what my character-building challenges did as well. He held summer intensives—multi-week retreats combining the physical labor of building the Farm's infrastructure with confrontation and "rapport" sessions. Students cleared brush, strung fencing, and dug (with pick and shovel) the foundation of a future community building. In confrontation sessions, Rose offered keen insight into the motivations and beliefs of his students and attacked these poses through humor and penetrating observations. In rapport sessions, his students sat in silence and let that silence deepen and pave the way for insights to arise. Through these and numerous other experiments, his students gained clarity and insight into their thought processes through backing away from falsehoods.

In time, a two-story brick building was construct-ed—one corner of a quadrangle envisioned as the heart of the TAT community. A large post-and-beam Chautauqua building was erected to hold public lectures. A barn was built for an expanding goat herd. A few students con-structed cabins and became permanent residents. Others started businesses in the local communities. Yet, as the years passed his most dedicated students from the early 1970s aged into their thirties. No one achieved enlighten-ment, and life marched on. Some decided to marry and have children, others searched for a new teacher and some simply came around less and less, until one day was their last. As the spiritual opening of the 1960s faded into the Reagan presidency of the 1980s, Rose presaged that a door was closed and a more materialistic era reigned.

By the time I met him on that cold March day, Mr. Rose was in his seventies, with a handful of "old timers" attending the quarterly TAT meetings. Both the brick community building and the Chautauqua building were relegated to storage sheds. Even the goat herd was reduced to a scraggly remnant barely visible through the weeds. Rose referred to us young college kids as "the last wave, and a rather small one at that."

While his history seemed innocuous enough, I continued to look for signs of a scam or evidence that Rose was simply deluded. It soon became stunningly clear he was not. We sat deep in discussion on Saturday afternoon. Normally the loudest person in a room, Augie was remarkably subdued around Rose, but finally spoke up. He launched into a long dissertation that contained a question somewhere in its midst. Rose at first listened intently, but then his attention appeared to drift and he straightened slightly in his seat. When Augie stopped, there was dead silence. At first, I waited for Rose to respond, but it became obvious this pause was purposeful. No one moved and no one spoke. Into this human silence, another more powerful quietude arose. I felt the room fill and vibrate with an energy at once intense and focusing, yet utterly quiet. Out of this pulsing silence these words appeared in my mind with complete conviction: "He knows." I have no idea how much time passed as we sat motionless on the edge of eternity. The intensity and focus started to fade, but I did not move, hoping to linger in the dimming spell. Finally, I could feel it no more, but still no one dared speak, until Rose cleared his throat and then began to talk.

Later I learned this event was the rapport that Rose referred to earlier. A profound presence seemed to emanate from him in that timeless moment. Some part of me responded to that feeling, and recognized it as what I was searching for. The vibrating stillness of the room was more real and more alive than anything previously experienced. The truth was real and palpable. Rose had it, but I didn't. I had a taste, but how could I get more?

Rose impressed me in other ways. Spry and funny, he took us on a lively tour of the Farm—hiking up and down hills like follow the leader. Rose was old, but he didn't seem *old*. He also seemed genuinely interested in being of help: letting a van load of strangers into his home, devoting a weekend to answering their questions and not charging a penny other than for food.

I returned to Raleigh ignited by this visit. Beyond challenging my self (again emphasizing *me* as separate from the *self* as an object to be studied) with character-building exercises, I sought something more, something deeper—a feeling of reality that I wanted to touch again. I did as little as possible to keep my graduate school funding intact, while I sat at my office desk filling a lab notebook with quotes from books like *In Search of the Miraculous* by Ouspensky, Rose's *Direct Mind Experience*, and *Lost in the Cosmos* by Walker Percy.

The quirks of my personality were fodder for many entries. In observing and reflecting on my personality, I noticed the lingering desire for a fast car, the hunger for sweets, the want of companionship, passing thoughts of superiority, concerns for clothing and appearance, and frustration at the lethargy of the mind when called to study its nature. Teasing out the motivations for my habits and reactions proved fascinating work, as I frequently seemed little more than a puddle of adopted, imposed, conflicting and ultimately pointless desires. Death was increasingly on my mind, as well. Ernest Becker's *The Denial of Death* confronted me with the utter meaninglessness of my actions when glimpsed through the lens of mortality—not just my death, but that of the planet and even the universe.

I started meditating regularly. Meditation was not the sort of action Augie talked about, so I turned to a book for instruction. I could have chosen a better first book, but it was what I had at hand. Precisely following the exercise, I closed my eyes and visualized an apple, then a spinning apple, and then an apple with a diamond it in. On a few occasions, the verbal thoughts in my mind stopped and whatever I visualized disappeared into a white light. These exhilarating moments sent chills through my body, but the experience was not the same as rapport.

Despite my rapport experience, despite my increasing efforts, and despite seeing the flaws in so much of my thinking, a part of me still held to my imagined future—a professor of soil science with a house in the country, a front porch swing, and a glass of lemonade. Every book, every SKS event, every meeting with Rose strengthened my conviction that I should commit entirely to the spiritual search, but I was still scared to let go.

Rose's path was not the idea of a well-balanced life with a bit of spiritual practice, some financial success, and a side-helping of a healthy relationship. What Rose modeled was a practice of total dedication to a single pursuit—leaving the old and familiar for the complete unknown—a one in a million shot at something called enlightenment. This business of subtraction was starting to get serious.

Rose offered no guarantees. Though Augie's entrepreneurial analogies for the seeker's life inspired me, Mr. Rose's path seemed austere. He recommended celibacy for his male students and believed sex was a drain on one's mental energy. As if that was not enough to dissuade the prospective seeker, Rose's stories from his early days were equally daunting. He spent winters in isolation in an unheated cabin so cold that he woke up one morning to find a mouse hunched over his nose warming itself. He fasted for days, and when he did eat, it was pots of rice with raisins thrown in for flavor. To my youthful eyes, Rose represented an ascetic life of meditation, frugality, and loneliness. Yet he also offered a glimmer of hope for finally being at peace in the world. Outwardly subtractive, but perhaps infinitely rewarding.

Here I stood, no longer completely hypnotized by the world of "big cigars and motorcars" as Doug liked to say, yet afraid to step off the ledge into the unknown. This high drama was in part my interpretation, as another part of me knew it was not that stark. "You don't have to give up anything," I wrote, "If you make your commitment to one thing, then that which gets in the way will be taken from you."

Yet I wavered until life intervened. In the early spring, I weighed quitting graduate school against a deeper commitment to the spiritual path. A group of ten SKS members planned to spend the summer at Mr. Rose's farm doing "serious" spiritual work. I was scheduled to spend the summer nursing corn and soybean research plots to gather data for my master's thesis. I wanted to go, but also wanted to hedge my bet with the security of a graduate degree and the old dreams it represented. "If you have a hedge," Augie warned, "you'll take it."

I wrote out lists of pros and cons, looked to my dreams for guidance and did all I could to unconsciously procrastinate a decision. I leaned towards leaving school, but the choice was still heavily on my mind when, on an evening in early May the phone rang and my brother told me that our dad passed away in his sleep. He was sixty-one years old, barely into his retirement from thirty years as a service technician with General Electric—a job he stuck with only for the security of its guaranteed pension. It was a crushing rebuttal of my hedging and a revelation of a family pattern of looking for a safe and secure way through life. Through the clarity of sorrow, it settled upon me that there were no guarantees, so why not try something remarkable?

Returning from the funeral in Kentucky, I stepped into the office of my major professor, dropped a few words about "death," "meaninglessness," and "purpose of life," then quit the program. Still as dour as the first day

I met him, he made no attempt to understand or dissuade and curtly dismissed me from his office. I was a cog in a machine, and now a broken cog needed to be replaced.

I wrote Mr. Rose a few days prior to quitting and explained my departure from school to spend the summer at his farm. A couple of days after leaving the professor's office, a small envelope arrived in the mail and Rose's response stunned me:

> I do not advise you to quit graduate school, because I do not know what that might entail in the long run. There are events that we commit ourselves to that we need to follow through on... but I do not know about reactions down the road. You can go to school and be celibate, you can go to school and get some esoteric books read on the side. But once school (a previous commitment) is over, then choose your life's commitment carefully and give it the same determination that you gave the school commitment.

His response struck me as reasonable, but I was no longer in a reasonable mood. Getting a few books read "on the side" was not enough. Determined, I called him the next day intent to do whatever needed to get to West Virginia. He patiently listened to my pleas, then explained that he never said I could not come, but wanted it to be my decision.

Something in me had responded to Rose's haunting presence, and as I wrapped up my research to pass on to another student, I walked the department halls in a peculiar state of detachment. What was once so important was now meaningless. Behind me, years of dreaming floated in the wake as I sailed forward hoping for a chance at enlightenment. I couldn't see I had exchanged one dream for another, but it didn't really matter. "There's garbage and stuff that smells worse than garbage," Rose said. Turning from one to the other was still backing away from untruth. Three weeks later, I sat on Mr. Rose's farm in a ramshackle building called the Emblem Lodge ready to do "serious" spiritual work for the summer.

Chapter 4:
The Natural Koan

"Who is controlling the machine?" Mr. Rose astutely said,
"You'll get enlightened before you find this out."

The Emblem Lodge was named after Dick Emblem, who no one remembered other than the fact that he was dead. This dubious memorial was a "lodge" in name only, being a wooden shack with tin siding, no plumbing, three bare light bulbs, and an interior wall paneled entirely in old doors… seen as either clever or disturbing depending on one's mood. Heavy wooden bunks with brokeback mattresses filled the interior. Light shone through cracks in the floor boards. Insects wailed outside in the summer heat. Rose kept the Farm rustic to discourage any "dharma bums" more interested in a vacation than the work of self-discovery. I judged him quite successful in this.

The Zen Den was vacated as Eric, Doug and Danny joined me, along with several other SKS members. Even Augie came along, though he stayed in a cabin separate from us college kids. While I anticipated a plan of action and schedule of activities, Rose casually appeared one morning and instead gave us two suggestions. The first was to spend no more than a half a day at physical work because it would stimulate the appetite and increased eating would drain the clarity from our thoughts (imagine post-Thanksgiving dinner). Second, he suggested learning hypnosis as a way to understand the mind. Beyond that he was available for advice, but would otherwise leave us to do as we pleased. With that thought, he walked away, leaving us to do just that.

Rose cautioned that whenever you made a commitment to something, "forces of adversity" would rise against you. I saw this again and again, but in more subtle forms than expected. Witness my next action: it's not that I intended to ignore Rose's advice, but one of the old-timers offered us work remodeling their store, and I found myself and several of my Zen-mates hammering nails on a hot roof completely contrary to Rose's suggestions. I didn't need the money, but it seemed silly to pass up the chance to make a few dollars. Fortunately, Augie pointed out the short-sightedness of earning chump change while Zen awaited. Sufficiently inspired, we all resigned from our nascent construction careers and resolved to stay on the Farm and keep focused. I topped that commitment by accepting Augie's invitation to stay at his cabin.

In contrast to Rose, Augie had no intention of letting me do as I pleased. Prior to this, my shyness kept me out of Augie's spotlight. Now however, the Farm's long summer days offered him little to do except shine that attention on me. Two liter of Diet Coke in hand, he set his sights on enumerating the numerous flaws in my character: I was a follower, I lacked initiative, I was insensitive, and I just wanted peace and quiet. I dodged each with some silent excuse. It was the day he confronted me for never sweeping the porch that finally broke through my denial. It was such a simple observation that it was hard for my mind to build the story of an excuse. Like a child, I assumed someone else would clean up after me. Despite my initial impulse to get mad and leave, I recognized nearly everything I felt Augie was harping on was true. I was immature, oblivious to other people, and self-centered.

What did any of this have to do with enlightenment? I can't say my deficient qualities prevented enlightenment, but can say those qualities helped keep me enamored of my self. They kept me laminated to my thoughts. They deafened me to those whose advice I needed. Those qualities kept the ego dancing, looking away from the signs of impermanence all around and within me.

Unlike my initial rejection of Augie's efforts, I secretly hoped for Mr. Rose to do more. Like Zen masters of ancient lore, Mr. Rose was capable of direct mind-to-mind transmission. He didn't talk about this much, but the old-timers in TAT did. While in contemporary Zen, transmission was reduced to a symbolic ceremony of the teacher acknowledging the student's understanding, with Rose it held the promise of a short-cut to enlightenment. Whether by fortuitous accident or by design, Rose might project his enlightenment experience into a student's mind. It sounded like fantasy, but I suspected Rose transmitted to us during that experience on my first trip to the Farm. Transmission and rapport were woven together in some way.

Ultimately, the idea of transmission was more of a distraction than a help. Some of his students stayed on year after year, long after their own spiritual efforts were reduced to nothing, in the hope that Rose might transmit to them—their worthiness proven by their loyalty to the guru, if nothing else. Rose said he couldn't hand us enlightenment on a platter, nor was the enlightenment success rate of his students—zero—encouraging. Even if he did transmit his enlightenment, he once warned it would be an "ersatz experience," like a shadow or a taste of his. It wouldn't be our own, but it might inspire us to strive on.

These warnings didn't dissuade me from scheming ways to hasten transmission. For example, Rose said that people of a similar "stature" had a natural rapport, as one might feel familiarity with a total stranger, and we would increase our stature by our spiritual efforts. While I didn't have Rose's stature, perhaps I could meet him halfway? A clear and focused mind, not filled with fear and thoughts of self-concern, might perceive the mind of another. Not literally reading another's thoughts, but feeling their nature. I suspected that my obliviousness to others which Augie pointed out was one of many detriments to rapport.

My hope for a short-cut to enlightenment was strengthened when Rose suggested a seven-day fast culminating in a rapport sitting. This must be the prelude to transmission, I thought, and this Herculean effort would separate the spiritual wheat from the chaff. To make sure no one died during the fast or snuck a bite of beef jerky, Rose had us partner up, so Danny and I settled into a small cabin at the edge of Rose's farm. Though without plumbing or even electricity, the cabin was a respite from the relative noise of Emblem Lodge and Augie's critiques. It was appropriately austere for two monks walling themselves into their cell for seven days.

Given his gifts as a storyteller, Danny's surprising intensity in the quiet art of meditation intimidated me. He, too, was ready to get serious, but even more so than me. My meditation practice had advanced from visualizing and concentrating on apples and diamonds, to observation of my mind. Danny was also deeply interested in watching the workings of his mind. To keep ourselves focused, Danny suggested we speak as little as needed and limit our reading. This gave me pause as reading occupied a large part of my days, but my sense of competitiveness forced me to agree.

The first day in our cabin, Danny staked out a spot on an old easy chair and his lean form and open-eyed gaze were astonishingly still. It was hot in the cabin, and without reading, talking, or eating to distract me, there was little to do except meditate. I focused on noticing my breathing: counting breaths one after another. As my attention drifted to daydreams, I forced it back to watching my breathing again and again, hour after hour. Though my mind wandered and tired of meditation, I refused to pick up a book unless Danny did too. He didn't break. On day two, I watched my attention lose focus yet again, then suddenly and effortlessly snap back to my breathing. I did nothing to make this happen. I realized that "I," the observer of my attention, was clearly separate from my attention! It was a fascinating discovery, yet paradoxically required intense concentration to recognize an automatic and effortless process.

By day three of the fast I was exhausted — a limp rag draped on a chair. Rather than meditating, my thoughts drifted uncontrolled. I had no interest in reading and no energy to observe my internal experience. By day five, even daydreaming was too much effort. At the end of day five, draped in the same chair, I realized that I might die if I did not stop. In a crystal clear moment of perception, I watched my mind decide not to stop. I saw this debate occur in my mind's eye, and saw it decided without input from the "me" who was watching. These thoughts I called "mine" were utterly robotic. Surprisingly, a state of extreme exhaustion rather than intense effort yielded this second glimpse of truth. Was this a prelude to enlightenment?

On day seven, Danny and I hobbled down to the farmhouse for the rapport sitting. Rose read some passages that I am sure were inspirational, but in my half-dead state they dropped into a deep well in which I sat at the very bottom. The sitting was as leaden as I felt, without a hint of the usual vibrant energy. As if surprised, Rose made the comment that we all seemed tired… Thus our spiritual marathon ended with no winners, and I dragged my body back up the hill, lost in thoughts of what would be my first meal.

In the way that one might have an insight from touching a hot stove, I appreciated the experience, but never again did a seven-day fast. While I found great value to moderating my food intake to free up time and avoid sleepiness after meals, I didn't like water-only fasting. Don't let my peculiar reaction prevent you from trying, however.

Like a pent-up sigh of relief, we burst forth from the Farm the following Friday night and landed at an all-you-can-eat Italian restaurant. Amidst the joys of garlic bread and pasta, we forgot any disappointments over the week-long fast and discussed plans for the coming school year. Most were leaving in the next few days to visit family before the start of school.

I chose to end the summer with a week in solitary retreat. Since transmission had failed, I'd break through to enlightenment on my own. "Isolation" was a tradition on Rose's farm, which meant spending anywhere from a weekend to a month in complete solitude. It was a time for deep introspection, and Rose recommended taking at most one book, so reading did not become a distraction. I was inspired by Rose's remark that pretty soon you realize that you are a machine, and then you want to know where the programming is coming from. That was exactly how the decision-watching experience in the cabin left me feeling—like a machine. Equally intriguing was Rose's tenet that the "view is not the viewer." I experienced this when seeing the attention and realizing it was separate from me as the observer. I wondered if the observer, as well, could be witnessed. Like placing my mind in an Escher drawing, could I watch myself watching myself? If possible, then which watcher could I claim as the real me? The answer to this would be a massive step on the subtractive path.

Perched on a hillside, my nine by twelve foot isolation cabin rested in the deep shade of tall poplars and oaks. Still, it was hot and stuffy, and the first day was most notable for the amount of napping. The naps mixed with eating, yoga, and about an hour of Vipassana meditation practice.

My guide to Vipassana was Joseph Goldstein's *The Experience of Insight*. The fundamental practice was attending to the breath. As thoughts or feelings arose, I labelled them quickly as "thinking, thinking" or "feeling, feeling," then went back to watching the breath. Ideally, by the time the labeling was done the thought or feeling had evaporated. More often though, something like this happened:

The sound of a bird brought an image of my grandfather's farm, which reminded me of a Sunday dinner with the family, and a cherry tree in their backyard, behind which was an old root cellar, which as a young boy I hesitantly ventured into. "Why am I so scared of new things?" I thought. "I've always been that way, and furthermore..." blah, blah and blah. Then as if waking from a dream, I recalled my intent to label thoughts and feelings and let them pass by the mind. And so it went.

The days were long, but punctuated by moments of time-stopping simplicity. Wraiths of steam hovered on the ground after a brief rain. Walking through this mist, I paused by a blackberry bush with branches drooping from the weight of berries. I took one, raindrops cleaving to its glistening black surface, and berry and rain dissolved in my mouth. I cared about nothing, and beauty arose amidst life stripped to its essentials. There was nowhere to be, and no one to be. I daydreamed of raising vegetables, cutting firewood, and hunting game in this primeval landscape.

More glimpses of the automatic and uncontrolled nature of thought occurred, and at times were unnerving. Sitting in meditation, thoughts floating by without effort, a sick, gut-level feeling would suddenly arise, as if I'd made a terrible and unrepairable mistake. Fear welled up and my mind turned away in a silent groan. As soon as my eyes opened the tension would subside. At its heart was the question, Who am I?

"Who am I?" wasn't a new question. All of the character-building work I had done with Augie and all of the retreating from erroneous views about my self, were aimed at discovering the truth about who I was. Yet those exercises focused on an exterior or personality-level view of my self. Though I didn't phrase it this way at the time, the feeling of this new inquiry was more about What am I?, rather than Who am I? "Who" implied there was a person, but "What" questioned the very nature of that so-called person.

By the end of the retreat, I hungered for an answer. I had found my natural koan, the question I had to solve, and the way to an answer was by looking directly at the mind through skillful meditation. This quiet art of meditation rather than Augie's emphasis on challenging the character was my new focus. I now had something previously unimaginable—a conscious connection to a deep longing. That longing was no longer masked behind dreams of front porches and lemonade. Instead, I saw that turning from those outward desires and journeying inward was the direct search for an answer to my question—subtraction was once again the way forward.

Chapter 5:
Choose a Direction

If I tell you to go five miles,
don't go one mile and then come back.

—*Richard Rose*

I had not, however, suddenly exchanged the cares of the world for full-time meditation. With the end of my summer "vacation," I returned to Raleigh to rejoin the SKS. Taking my time, I stopped at a crowded overlook in the Shenandoah Valley, squeezed my way to the railing, and quietly took in the valley's sun-dazzled breadth. For a few seconds there existed nothing but calm space, as my sense of self expanded and dissolved into the still, nameless vista before me. The restless mind quickly singled out a barn, then a copse of trees and tourists with cameras in hand. These pieces broke the nameless whole into chunks, objects identified and claimed, and the stillness was scattered like a jigsaw puzzle. The moment seemingly gone, I walked back to my car basking in this glimpse of another way of seeing the world.

Some miles later, this blessing was interrupted by a dimly burning red warning light on the dashboard of my car. A sudden rush of thoughts pushed all else out of my mind: Was my battery failing? Was the alternator dying? The valley's beauty was forgotten in a swarm of concern. Afraid the car would not start if I turned it off, I gassed up and made the rest of the trip to Raleigh without stopping—driven by worry, the epitome of Walker Percy's image of a "little traveling suck of care, sucking care with him from the past and being sucked to towards care in the future."

While the summer with Rose inspired me to turn inward and study the mind, there were several external considerations demanding attention. The SKS was growing more popular, as Augie's mix of Zen and self-improvement found an audience. The Zen Den residents reunited, joined several new roommates, and rented a large apartment which we unanimously christened... the Zen Den. The new apartment meant bills to pay, and I was no longer a student so needed a job in the "real world."

Using work as spiritual practice appealed to me. While meditating for a living would have been nice, if I had to spend eight hours a day at a job, I could find something that challenged me, helped to overcome my self-centeredness, revealed beliefs, and improved my intuition.

Augie thought work should test one's character and hone the mind and no better arena existed for that task than sales. With no work experience, retail seemed an easy place to start. I bluffed my way through interviews at assorted shops, but with looks ranging from bemused to confused, it was clear they all wondered why a soil science drop-out was looking to sell hot tubs or mattresses. With Doug's assurance that I was a natural at selling death, I successfully interviewed for a funeral consultant job. Yet nothing was particularly appealing until Belle, a new attendee at the meetings at Augie's place, described waiting tables. She explained food service was relatively physical work that was not mentally draining, offered a flexible schedule, and paid based on performance. She suggested I apply at the Darryl's restaurant where she worked, which gave me pause.

Belle was attractive, and the fact I noticed that revealed that while once afraid of being alone, I was now afraid of getting entangled. Rose's recommendation of celibacy was relatively easy for me, and I did not want any stumbles, so I side-stepped her invitation and applied at a Darryl's on the other side of town.

Even the manager at Darryl's was suspicious of my situation. Rather than hiring me as a waiter, he gave me a two week trial as a food runner, which basically meant delivering food from the kitchen to the customer's table. I appeared for work precisely as instructed: black shoes, black pants, an all-cotton white shirt with medium starch, and a pure silk tie. I looked like a waiter, but my first night as a food runner enveloped me in a fog of war. Clutching a map of the restaurant tables, I ran barbeque ribs and flaming-hot fajitas from kitchen to customers in an endless round. Large men and even larger women inhaled glasses of Coca Cola faster than I refilled them. Tables were piled with dirty dishes, hostesses glared at me, and thirsty patrons tried to catch my eye. Surrounded by food, but starving, I nibbled on left-over crackers while hiding in the wait station. This was my foxhole amidst the chaos. Home at midnight, I propped my feet in an easy chair and nodded off. I seriously doubted the spiritual value of this employment exercise.

At the end of my two weeks, the manager sat me down for a heart-to-heart and said, "You need to show some personality or else we have to let you go." Don't just drop a customer's food and run, he said. Engage with them, ask them how they like their food, say *something*! With this warning, he anointed me a waiter and sent me forth into the wilds.

Determined to live the SKS spirit and not crumble in the face of adversity, I forced my introverted self to interact. Waiting tables proved excellent therapy. I was faced, again and again, with seeking the perspective of the customer in the moment: to discover their needs, listen, and serve. I battled the self-centeredness Augie pointed out, and at some level tried to find rapport. Not the mystical connection of Rose's rapport, but a precursor to that which was consideration of another person and basic human understanding. In the beginning, my attempts were clumsy and feigned. "Fake it till you make it," one friend advised.

Like a visitor from outer space, I watched and learned from other wait staff: What was something quick and funny I could say? Which tables wanted you to chat and which wanted to be left alone? As the weeks passed, my performance livened and gained spontaneity. The feedback was precise because if people liked me, they left a good tip. Though the restaurant threatened to slide into anarchy every Friday and Saturday night, those were the lucrative shifts which I simultaneously wanted and shied away from. I preferred a lazy Monday lunch where a few business people trickled in, but such shifts paid a pittance. Once again, I faced the tension of fear and desire.

One Friday evening, I rushed through the noisy kitchen to the walk-in cooler in quest of condiments. As the door slammed behind me, the sharp contrast between the cold, deep quiet of the cooler and the hot madness of the kitchen was so profound that my mind tripped into an altered experience. Suddenly all was perfect. I was unburdened of every need to be anything. I felt so relieved, so free, that laughter arose. Stepping into the kitchen again, it was momentarily transformed from a stampede to a whirling, easeful dance. In the time it took to cross the kitchen to the restaurant floor, the feeling faded, but I took this experience as a glimpse of progress.

While never comfortable at anything faster paced than lazy lunch shifts, I moved through the ranks till assigned section sixteen. Furthest from the kitchen, yet with more seating capacity than other sections, it was a money-maker if handled well and loomed like my personal Everest. I blundered there weeks earlier, so sufficiently neglecting six middle-aged women that they complained to the manager. This night, though, I felt happiness and ease: running trays up the stairs, filling drinks, and joking with customers. This was the culmination of a remarkable experiment. I chose a job to stretch my psychological boundaries and it did—forcing me to think in new ways and change my behavior in order to succeed. The job provided the opportunity and the necessary incentive for me to expand the edges of my introverted and fearful shell.

At the same time, nothing was different. What kept me from enlightenment? I saw my personality, I manipulated it into new contortions, new experiences, new relationships, yet could not see past it. Who am I? What was my true nature?

While I was at the restaurant, the SKS kept growing. Like a missionary, Bill moved to Chapel Hill and started a group at the University of North Carolina. Augie divided his time between N.C. State, Chapel Hill, and the Friday night meetings. Building and sustaining these groups took an increasing amount of work. "Poster wars" raged as we stapled and taped meeting announcements over two campuses. We implanted our members in places of influence like stealthy revolutionaries. One became head of the N.C. State lecture series, and he funneled money to events co-sponsored by the SKS such as parapsychology researchers from the Stanford Research Institute, and Augie's *Five Years with a Zen Master* talk. Another member infiltrated the community access TV station and soon SKS-sponsored lectures were broadcast locally.

This "group work" was inspiring and challenging, and commitment to growing the groups was increasingly seen as a measure of commitment to the spiritual search. Stepping up to the plate, I volunteered to organize a lecture given by near-death researcher Dr. Kenneth Ring. The lecture was a success, but I wondered again if enlightenment was any closer. Yes, it took a lot of effort and stretched my abilities, but in what way was I "reversing the vector?" Was putting up posters going to get me enlightened? I saw little interest from Augie in the sort of introspection I did on Rose's farm. His focus was to drive members to grow the groups. Were we committed to helping each other find the truth, or were we cogs in yet another machine? My summer at Rose's farm had me questioning not just who I was, but what constituted spiritual work.

Amidst this whirl, Belle and I continued to talk. My tactical decision placed me in a restaurant across town from hers, but Belle moved within a stone's throw from the Zen Den. My plan for avoiding women unraveled as she frequently stopped by to ask a question or drop off a little gift of food. She was persistent in a kind and gentle way. These gestures grew into long talks about spirituality. Her perceptive abilities reminded me of Augie, but while I questioned and fought Augie's few critiques of me, Belle's observations were delivered in such a guileless tone that I considered them. She observed that I liked people who were useful, that I did not trust others because I hid my own thoughts and emotions, and that my intuition (and all of my connection to feeling) was hampered because my love was conditional. These conversations proved as mind-opening as my first SKS meetings. This intimacy was new territory for me, and I was like a turtle peeking out of its shell. "You can't be too open," I told myself, "You have to be careful in this world."

On a breezy fall day, Belle and I went for a walk in one of Raleigh's old and elegant cemeteries. It was our first time away from the Zen Den together—if not an actual date, at least date-like. As we walked, shafts of sunlight broke through darkening clouds while the wind picked up energy from an afternoon storm. We paused under a tree as big drops of rain splattered our clothes. Suddenly a gust struck the tree, blowing off a mass of burnt orange leaves like seeds from a dandelion. Belle ran after them, laughing, and I instinctively followed, pulled forward into a beautiful unknown. There was a faint, and long-forgotten, sense of play and wonder that was the opposite of pushing and challenging my personality, yet equally powerful. The leaves scattered before us, impossible to catch. Giving up the chase, Belle turned and I looked down at her, relaxing into the cool rain soaking my clothes. Beauty rose up from every pore of the world to greet and hold me for a few splendid seconds. A week later, we confessed our deep feelings for one another.

I was in quite the jam now, stuck between desire and desire, or fear and desire, or fear and fear. "You can't carry your girlfriend on your back to enlightenment," Rose warned, and Augie frowned upon the complications of relationships. Indeed, there was an unspoken assumption that you did not date within the SKS groups. I, too, did not want to fall in love again. I wanted something different—a way to be in a relationship yet not have the quest for enlightenment give ground to a quest to cling to another person. I feared the gravitational pull of obsession: my mind drifting toward thoughts of my partner, daydreaming of the future, worrying what she thought, trying to read her mind and anticipate her wishes. I did not want to return to that way of being.

Against these fears, Belle and I hoped the "either/ or" of romance or enlightenment would become "both/ and." We did not know if our path together was "right" or "wrong," "spiritual" or "not spiritual." We deeply desired an answer to our spiritual questions, and freely told one another if we felt distracted. We were celibate, and not once did we go on a proper date. Instead, we talked of books, intuitions and dreams, and shared notes on meditation. Our relationship straddled a line between the romantic and platonic.

Belle was as determined as me to find answers to her spiritual longing and decided to move to Rose's farm.

The ripple of astonishment through the SKS was palpable. While finding students for Mr. Rose was the original point of the group, for someone to actually leave the SKS to work with Rose was disconcerting, and it disconcerted me to notice the disconcertment! I suspected some even resented Belle's decision, as she had done little to support the SKS daily affairs. Instead, she bypassed the group work and went straight to Rose. Belle's boldness confront-ed me and inspired greater efforts... and darker moods.

Extraordinarily aware of how my time was spent, I wanted every hour devoted to spiritual work. Feeling stuck, I doubled-down on the seriousness quotient, and divided life into the "not spiritual" and the "spiritual." In my mind, I kept a running criticism of other group members who laughed and joked too frequently and I branded them "not serious." Equally critical of myself, a single distracted meditation spiraled into feeling hopeless. If not actually wasting time, I worried about wasting time. On top of this tight grip, a pronouncement from Rose rattled the SKS. He said we should go "all out" on the spiritual life for three years, then we would know what our potential was. The normally reticent Zen master cast forth a challenge. It was a sign that now was the time for great action.

I piled on more activities: keeping a dream journal, taking up Rose's suggestion to practice hypnosis and conducting experiments in ESP. I visited a Jungian therapist and sat with the channeler of a disincarnate Zen

Master. Still dogged by the fatigue that appeared in my first months of graduate school, I drafted my roommate Alex to go running with me and spur my body to greater health and productivity. The Zen Den residents sat in rapport every week. The Zen master called for more, yet none of this work and flurry seemed enough. Ever again, my natural koan would call to me: Who and what was this "I" making all of this noise?

One thing I didn't want to do more of was SKS marketing. While Augie once intended to introduce students to Rose, now I felt Augie intended to build a group that matched his own vision of the spiritual life. I was not alone in this thought, and a quiet schism developed between the more contemplative SKS members and those engaged with testing their character through the business of running the group. The past summer of meditation, fasting, reading, and solitary retreat pulled at me, making the task of organizing events and expanding the influence of the SKS increasingly onerous. I hungered for the "real work": To look directly at my mind with my mind and attempt to see what was behind the curtain of thoughts.

I volunteered for fewer SKS assignments, until I was absent from even the menial task of postering. There was no decisive confrontation with Augie and no grand exit. While some thought I was chasing Belle, when I announced I was moving to Rose's farm most realized I desired to further my search for truth. Even I wondered about the wisdom of thinking an old man on a ramshackle farm in West Virginia had more to offer than the rising opportunities forged by Augie.

I had no plan as to how long I would stay with Rose, but reasoned the SKS would be here when I returned. Rose, however, had only a short time to help me and now was the moment to strike. It was evening when I turned at the Hare Krishna sign and drove the winding route past the Krishna temple. I passed onto the gravel road at the McCreary Ridge cemetery and, five hundred feet further, pulled off this pot-holed and dusty road and into Rose's world. He sat in a faded, rusting green metal chair underneath the enormous sycamore tree that dominated the side yard of his farmhouse. At first Mr. Rose did not know who I was, or that I intended to move into the Emblem Lodge, but then he either remembered or simply accepted the fact that I was here to stay.

"You must perfect yourself," he said, "choose a direction and become a vector in that direction."

Thus, my life in West Virginia began.

Chapter 6:
Outhouse Zen

Rose said, "What causes enlightenment is the agony within the man. There is no formula or rules which can be written out."
"I need more agony," I said.
He just laughed.

Mr. Rose's one hundred and twenty acres were about as isolated as one needed to get from the distractions of life. The quiet was broken by two recurring strains: the wafting rhythms of Hare Krishna chanting from the nearby temple and the droning ventilation fan of a distant coal mine. Rose charged fifty dollars a month for a bunk in the Emblem Lodge. With no debt, no phone, and no health insurance, I could have lived there for years as a full-time seeker. I just wanted to learn all I could from Rose. Spry as he seemed on my first visit, Rose remarked that he didn't have many years left as a teacher.

Despite moving to his farm, Rose did not change his approach with me. There were no assignments or plans of action. "Get yourself a book," he said "and spend some time alone in one of the cabins. If you run into any trouble come see me."

The Farm was hardly bustling with activity I needed to isolate from. Belle was staying with Rose and his family and had forewarned me in a letter that she was, for now at least, fully occupied in working with Mr. Rose. I wanted to see her, but would never ask her to do something she felt was a distraction from her path. Of the residents I met in my first visits, all but one had moved away. That last man standing was Art, who lived in a rickety, bat-infested trailer next to the farmhouse. Fifty-something, he'd moved from Florida to help take care of the Farm. Always ready with a smile, he seemed to enjoy my companionship, yet never needed it. Despite the proximity, I went days without seeing him unless I choose to knock on his door. Rose and his family generally only visited on weekends, as they had another house in the nearby town of McMechen. Nevertheless, I followed Rose's advice and began planning a thirty-day solitary retreat.

Solitude called to me though I did not fully understand its promises and hazards. Stashed under my bunk was a copy of *The Wisdom of the Desert* by Thomas Merton. Though I was 1,500 years removed by time, religion, and place, I felt a kinship with the Desert Fathers. They were hermits of the Middle Eastern deserts. "What the Fathers sought most of all was their own true self, in Christ," Merton explained, "And in order to do this, they had to reject completely the false, formal self, fabricated under social compulsion in 'the world.'" The Fathers did not flee from the world because of fear or failure. It was a conscious rejection, a backing away from untruth which led them to the desert. I was certain Rose knew of these men. Standing on the dusty gravel road one afternoon, I told him about my isolation plans. "In the past," Rose said, "if a guy wanted some answers, he would go out into the desert and fast until he got them," he paused and looked up the hill towards the weather-beaten Lodge, "This place is like a desert."

I look back upon that thirty-day isolation like a slowly unfolding disaster. First, I discovered a pair of wrens nesting in the cabin's stovepipe. Far from quiet woodland animals, they flew in and out of the metal stovepipe every few minutes, scraping the metal sides like fingernails across a blackboard. At each visit the babies erupted in cheeping. For two days I tried to ignore it, reasoning that any skilled meditator could maintain focus through the racket. I couldn't. I plucked the nest from the pipe and placed it in a tree a few feet away. I knew little of birds and was incredulous when the parents kept returning to the pipe. I moved the nest next to the pipe to no effect. More days of noise awaited if I returned the nest to the pipe, but if I did not the babies would die. It seemed my only choice was to abandon the isolation or leave the birds to die.

They died.

I was more angry than sorry at the time. Angry with myself and the universe. Angry to see a world filled with endless collisions of robotic desires. "What's good for the picnic is not good for the pig," Rose once wryly commented. I am sorry about the birds today.

Silence restored, I grimly embarked on a course of intense Vipassana practice. I meditated in forty-five minute blocks with an hour or so rest in between. Within three days, my right knee hurt from kneeling in meditation and pain in my left shoulder woke me during the night. A month began to seem like a lot of days to watch the ramblings of the mind, and my body, mind, and what seemed like the entire world raised a protest.

On the fourth day, I walked from the cabin to the Lodge and looked down the hill towards the farmhouse and the road leading to town. Out there were people and activity—all that gave life meaning. Behind me was the emptiness of the woods. I felt like a castaway, separated from the world by an ocean of my own creation. Utterly alone; utterly lost.

Though I wavered, I did not break and run. In search of a respite from the cabin walls, I walked deeper into the woods. Far from relaxing, every one of God's creatures seemed intent to sting, bite, or nest on me. The deer flies were the worst. They circled just out of harm's reach, then dove in for a bite. Swirling a towel around my head kept them at bay, but I must have looked like a madman dancing through the woods. There was no comfort to be found.

Rather than profundities, my journal filled with escapist daydreams: businesses to start, conversations with Belle, restaurant dinners, books, physical fitness plans, and even acts of violence.

Rather than ramp up my meditation time, I cut it. Focusing for more than a few minutes became impossible. I made other discoveries, though. I found peace of mind in a big bowl of spaghetti—as a wash of carbohydrates drowned out any observation of mind. I learned there was a limit to how many hours one can sleep in a day. I tallied my routines like a repentant monk: sleeping eight and a half to nine hours, eating one hour, two hours walking and bathing, two to three hours reading, dozing one hour, meditating three hours and daydreaming five. Rather than being freed from thoughts, I watched them run unobstructed through my mind.

I celebrated day fifteen with an ascetic's feast: a can of tuna, and a bowl of corn flakes cereal with warm, powdered milk. My mental and physical fatigue was nearly overwhelming, and I berated myself for laziness, weakness, and any other deficiency I conjured in comparison to other seekers—all of whom were certainly Olympian meditators with unwavering focus. Counting my breaths was not one iota easier than in Raleigh, and I doubted all the reasons for moving. I fantasized about escape, leaving the dreary life of a seeker to become, of all things, a baker.

In the midst of this slow mental unraveling, I decided to fast for five days. Maybe this would reset my seriousness and focus. Piling fatigue on top of fatigue, I waited out the fast and did little more than record my dreams each day. By the end of the fast, I just wanted out.

Despite the misery I hung on. While it made little rational sense to continue this failure, the SKS instilled in me the value of keeping commitments. Keeping a commitment was a statement of energy applied in a direc-tion—the vector that Rose said we must become. Though I did not leave, my discipline in all other areas collapsed. I rummaged through the cabin and unearthed a 1200-page hardback called *The Rise and Fall of the Third Reich*. As if a military scholar, I methodically read it cover to cover and rejoiced in the distraction.

As the final days of isolation crept by, I reflected on all that went wrong, as well as what I hoped to do in the coming months. I developed a list of goals: exercise and eat more, learn to speak up and not worry about looking like a fool, find a new mental discipline, and try one day of isolation a month. Despite the fatigue and discomfort, the struggles with meditation, and killing baby birds, I was not depressed.

I walked out of the woods on a Monday morning and knocked on Art's door. It was warm in his trailer, and I heard the faint rustling of bats behind the wood paneling. I took his offered chair, then watched as my mind stepped over a small hurdle of silence and hesitantly spoke my first words in thirty days. At first, it was like watching a movie with no idea what words would happen next, but then the dialogue began to feel like a part of me. Later that day, I drove into town to pick up fresh groceries. After the relative stillness of the woods, the motion of cars and people was hypnotizing. Perhaps this was what a baby felt watching a mobile spin above its crib. In the grocery, the music playing on the store loudspeaker was as much of a treat as the fresh apples I bought.

To a large degree it was my SKS "training" that kept me from quitting. A kind of stubbornness born of pride in keeping my word. It also helped to be very clear about what I was committing to and why, and acknowledge that doubts would inevitably arise. In comparison, two visitors at the Farm arrived shortly before my isolation. One started a two week fast, but ended it on day two. The other started an isolation, but left early. Did they hold their word of lessor value than I did? I doubt they thought so. More likely they were victims of thoughts they believed to be their own.

What were the thoughts that convinced them to leave? Likely not daydreams of quitting to become bakers. Such daydreams were relatively easy to recognize as dead ends and passing fancies. The simpler thoughts were more insidious. "I'll be better prepared next time," seemed a reasonable thought when in pain. The next reasonable thought was, "I should quit." Those were the thought trains that wrecked commitments. Did that mean I should never second guess my commitments, or that I should ignore pain? I didn't have a choice, really. Pain and discomfort would arise, and thoughts of second guessing would arise. Seeing that gave some space between the first thought and the reaction to it, and in that space there was room to notice a new thought or feeling—like recalling the reasons for my commitment, or noticing a sliver of peace in the space between thoughts.

Shortly after my isolation, Alex decided to leave school and move from Raleigh to the Farm. My former running buddy was big-hearted and thoughtful to the point of neglecting his own needs. Despite my desire for solitude, I was happy at his arrival and life at the Farm settled into a new routine.

The typical day involved rising with the sun, taking a few minutes to record any dreams, then a breakfast of raisin bran with dried milk. Next was a couple of hours of reading. I kept handwritten notes on a separate sheet of paper for each book, copying inspiring lines, and record-ing questions and comments about particular passages. Morning was my most energetic period, so I meditated as well. Lunch was a peanut butter and jelly sandwich, corn chips, and an apple. Lethargic afternoons were for physical activity: sweeping the wooden floor of the Lodge, carrying water from the spring down the hill, or a walk. Dinner was rice or pasta with frozen mixed vegetables. Evening brought more reading, as well as time for conversation with Alex. Our minds complemented each other well, with just enough difference in perspective to keep surprising each other. The conversations veered from questions to ask Rose, small talk about our childhood, to our favorite pastime of dreaming up inventions. There was no television, radio, phone, newspapers, or magazines. We were both there to do one thing, and each day was mine to use as best as I could in a self-directed search for truth.

Life never stopped its challenges. As the trees erupted in their fall colors, Alex and I belatedly realized we needed a mountain of firewood to keep the drafty Lodge warm day and night. To accomplish that we had a single, rusted bow saw, so dull that we christened it the "Zen saw." We dragged in fallen branches and worked up a sweat cutting what amounted to a few toothpicks. What we needed were logs and lots of them. A local TAT member took pity on our frozen doom and brought his chainsaw to fell two dead locust trees. Before he could cut the trees up for firewood, Rose promptly banned him from the Farm for cutting trees without permission. Though I considered Rose's age might have affected his judgment, ultimately I decided this was a Zen-like attack on the ego. I couldn't vouch for the effectiveness of that, but Mr. Rose did effectively foil our plans for winter warmth.

Ironically, in the two months since moving to the Farm, Belle was far from a part of my daily routine. We had not spoken since my arrival, though I occasionally glimpsed her when visiting Rose at his home in McMechen. Through the Farm's tiny grapevine of gossip, I heard that Rose worked intensively with her, and she spent half her time in tears. I couldn't imagine what this was like, nor did I want any part of Rose's confrontation. Whether his legendary attacks on the ego were all an act, I did not know, but I did know that even Augie withered under Rose's unrelenting gaze.

Belle got another dose of Rose's Zen when he told her to move out of his house. She found a small apartment in Moundsville and frequented Rose's house like a stray puppy despite her banning; determined to get his help. Her apartment gave us the chance visit and exchange stories of our spiritual adventures. Despite my questions, I never figured out how exactly Rose was working with her. Belle superstitiously guarded that work and felt that talking about a process before it was finished could ruin it.

Though completely chaste we endeavored to keep our interactions hidden, lest Rose find some reason to doubt my spiritual intentions and kick me off the Farm. I never felt guilty about our visits, as I felt our relationship was misunderstood rather than inappropriate or wrong in the context of our spiritual search. Belle's apartment wasn't even a great distraction. It was actually slightly less comfortable than the Lodge. She had no money for furniture and little for heat, so we sat on the floor in our jackets and talked over a simple dinner of scrambled eggs and sausage.

One afternoon, Belle and I nestled on the floor under a pile of blankets. I stared at the ceiling and soaked in the feelings of being alive: the heart effortlessly beating, my breath moving in and out, seeing, hearing, and the myriad processes, happening automatically, that kept me alive. This tiny speck of me, laying on the floor of a room, spinning through space on a mote of a planet within the wisp of a galaxy, within other interstellar clouds all residing within an unimaginable vastness, all residing in a moment called "time." My mind drifted back into the room, where it was pleasantly warm under the covers, and the comfort of being next to Belle was palpable and satisfying. "This is what I always wanted," I thought. Someone who loved me and I loved them. My attention shifted more deeply inside and there was the prick of uncertainty. A silent groan of dissatisfaction rent the comfort of the moment. Though surrounded by all I wanted, at the core I had no clue what I was, what any of this meant, or what happened when I died. At core, I was as unknown and unimaginable as the vastness of the universe. The hollowness I felt inside simultaneously seemed like an enormous pit behind me with my heels close to its edge—a great, empty space threatened to swallow me. Despite this, clearly some part of me still hoped that a woman and a normal life would save me, that somehow I was different from every human being that ever lived—that I could cheat death and play at life forever.

The Way of Subtraction is not easy or certain. Some desires aren't so much let go as they wither and die..

Though Rose suspected I would fall off the celibacy wagon, I was far more concerned with the minutia of whether or not a particular conversation with Belle met my criteria of spiritual worthiness. Was I wasting time? Was my attachment to her keeping me from enlightenment? We met for Christmas shopping one afternoon, and as she showed me sweater after sweater I felt my life slipping away. I was a dying man spending my last hours looking at clothes. I wanted nothing to do with this world of shiny baubles. I got quiet and withdrawn, refusing to tell her what I felt. All she knew was that something was wrong, that it must have something to do with her, so I must be planning on leaving. Which I was, in the back of my skull, because that temporarily seemed an easier solution than finding the courage to articulate what I felt. Despite my periodic meltdowns over the spiritual worth of our relationship, we managed to see each other nearly every week for a few hours of conversation and caring for one another.

My life as a full-time seeker took on a never quite comfortable pattern: spending days on the Farm reading and meditating, slowly sinking into despair as I lost the thread connecting me to my deep desire, then running to Rose for a dose of inspiration. About once a week Alex and I went to McMechen, where Rose welcomed us into his kitchen and offered a cup of tea or strong coffee. Compared to the Farm, his McMechen house was bright and cheery, which I attributed to Cecy's influence. It was also relatively warm. We settled around the kitchen table, and Alex and I unrolled our list of questions.

Rose continued to be both extremely practical and magically enigmatic. Our questions often yielded a story rather than a direct answer. Telling of a farmer he worked for as a young man, Rose's eyes gleamed as he described this frugal Scotsman loading a hay wagon. Trying to conserve his strength, the farmer would stumble forward with a pitchfork full of hay, using his body's momentum to reach the wagon. It crossed my mind this was a parable pointing at my own frugality and Scotch nature, but it was also damned funny as Rose reenacted the scene. My troubles faded in the warmth of his kitchen and presence. My questions and frustrations evaporated and the way became clear. There was hope for finding an answer and finding it was the only real task before my life. Rose did not inspire by exhorting us to try harder. Instead, his solid presence was like a lighthouse—pointing in a direction to which my soul responded and said "Yes, *that* is what is most important." As that feeling arose, my few remaining questions lost their significance. I was ready to return to the Farm and get to work meditating and reading.

Not that I thought reading would give me an answer. While I took numerous notes, the main benefit I saw was that reading kept my mind focused on the search. Where my energy and time went was where I saw progress. Like feeding a fire, this new material led to moments of inspiration where I drew a connection between two dissimilar ideas or paused to reflect on a new thought. Reading also led to action by exposing me to new practices which kept my mind engaged and exploring. For example, reading *On the Way to Satori*, a book I've now long forgotten, led me to experiments with prayer.

It would have been tough without Rose. The winter sky was gray and shrouded for days on end. It was hard to stay inspired and energetic. When I did get inspired and ready to work, the amorphous nature of the problem immediately confronted me. Who am I? What is awareness? Where does thought come from? These questions offered nothing to grab hold of, and no program of exercises to lead me to an answer. I only had the mind to look at the mind. As the first snow arrived, I silently directed my frustrations at Alex, whom I alternately resented for interfering with my solitude, then felt blessed to share my thoughts with.

Days before Christmas, Danny abandoned the Raleigh Zen Den and took the bunk above mine. Danny was even more intense than during last summer's fast. Unsleeping, he lay in his bunk the majority of each day without speaking. He was looking at a different world, or seeing something I did not, and his haunted quality grew even stronger. When he finally joined us for dinner or a conversation around the wood stove, it was like he just walked in from combat and I saw his mind refocusing to fully engage with the room. He was clearly more serious than me, and actually meditating rather than dwelling on the same thoughts day after day. I drove myself into depression through comparison with Danny's hot pursuit.

By mid-January, my ball of resentment was piled up like the deepening snow. I skipped going into town with Alex and Danny to see Mr. Rose, as compared to Danny I was obviously too weak to muster the determination needed for enlightenment. I festered on the Farm, biding my time till the day Mr. Rose came to see me, at which point I planned to ambush him with a tirade of complaints and an undeniable list of the deficiencies which prevented my spiritual attainment. After days of daydreaming my case, I finally spied Mr. Rose's brown van parked at the farmhouse. Trudging down the hill, I made a final review of my frustrations. Rose was outside, and I asked if we could talk. "Sure," he said, and plunged us across a field of foot and a half deep snow and down to the Chautauqua building. Neither of us said a word as we huffed and puffed through the snow. It was just me and the Zen master, and my emotions were a wordless whirl inside me.

We broke through the snow and into the gloom of the Chautauqua building's enormous meeting space. Dust-covered pews facing a low podium attested that no events had been held here for years. Rose puttered about the building, looking over the assorted junk squirreled away in the shadowy recesses. He did not ask me what was wrong, he did not whirl around and slap me with a Zen koan. He just waited. I broke the silence with a jumble of words—pouring out my frustrations, my lack of passion, my doubt and dark despair—which peaked in a heartfelt confession that "If I could think of someplace to go, I would. I'd leave."

As I said those final words, my frustration began to disintegrate in the knowledge that there was nowhere to go and nothing to do except keep trying. Rose, who continued to putter about the building throughout my soul-baring, quietly laughed, then directed my attention to a looming antique armoire. He did not speak a word in response, yet my resentments were gone—as if absorbed by the void, the depth of Rose's presence, the silence of the Chautauqua building, or the true desire suddenly clear within me. Nothing had changed; I had no more of a plan as to what to do or how to get enlightened than I did when I walked down the hill. Yet, my mood lifted and now the goal seemed tangible and possible. The details of how to get there did not matter. All that mattered was I once again knew what was most important.

In the following days, winter deepened around my momentary inspiration and a siege mentality descended as we started rationing wood. Reinforcements arrived when Mike C. also moved to the Farm. He was an older TAT member whose cabin Danny and I stayed in during our summer fast. Mike felled a large locust tree for us, but it was down a snow-covered hill far from the Lodge. With Danny in isolation, Alex and I turned a broken sheet of plywood into a makeshift sled, and strapped ourselves to it with rope. The frigid air burned our lungs as we dragged and pushed the log-laden sled through snow that spilled over our boots. Sweating and cold, thighs burning, Alex and I started laughing. How did we wind up like this? I fell back into the snow, suddenly quiet except for the sound of our breath. The sun shone. The sky was emerald blue. This was all so ludicrous. Zen.

One morning, it was twenty-three degrees below zero and the water in the cup next to my bunk froze solid. The Lodge had a makeshift sink which simply drained onto the ground through a straight pipe running through the floor. That froze too, so we periodically poured boiling water down the drain. Our heat-retaining efforts grew more inventive: we laid down carpet remnants to cover the gaps in the floor and stapled carpet pad to the door. We partitioned the forty foot length of the Lodge with plastic sheeting thumb-tacked to the ceiling and covered the windows with the same. What was left was a dimly lit life pod of warmth.

Like cuckoo-clock figurines, Danny came out of isolation and I went in. Despite the frustration and cold, my journal revealed evolving thoughts: "Somehow the answer lies in not this-not that; plus and minus simultaneously... but it is like looking at the night sky trying to comprehend infinity." Such thoughts left my mind quiet, as if awaiting a response.

Winter was a wonderful time for a solitary retreat. The tiny cabin's woodstove was comforting: snapping and crackling, with waves of heat radiating from its black metal sides. I was finally warm! I carefully managed my food, eating just enough to keep from feeling hungry, yet not so much that I got sleepy. While meditating, the thought arose "Just say it." I knew exactly what to say: "I can do it," I said aloud. Enlightenment was possible. The insight came that, "I can't locate the source of my thought because I am thought." That I was only thought and nothing more carried disturbing implications that danced at the edge of my consciousness. Could it be that my sense of identity was built of sand? Though I did not have answers, these questions marked progress.

Our tiny community grew yet again when Bob F. moved from Colorado. Bob cleaned out a run-down trailer next to the Lodge, running an extension cord for power and cutting a hole through the thin metal siding for the pipe of a wood stove. I was certain this jack-leg affair would ignite in flames, but Bob survived my dire prediction. With our numbers tripled, Rose talked of having regular weekly meetings. We met once and had high hopes for a rapport session, but instead Rose told stories and then he left. I was still waiting for Rose to lead us to enlightenment. Maybe Rose thought we were not ready for rapport sittings, but he also seemed increasingly forgetful. Was he no longer capable of leading?

Despite the new blood, winter slowly froze us in lethargy. The cold and the snow continued unabated. Warming my hands over a pot of boiling water one morning, I stared outside at the knee deep snow. Behind me, Danny and Alex appeared dead in their bunks. I piled on long underwear, wool pants, a shirt, sweater, coat, cold weather cap, bandana, wool glove inserts, leather palm gloves, wool socks and insulated boots, and went outside to build a snowman. It was a pointless activity, but at this point so was everything. Roused from hibernation, Alex and Danny joined me, then Mike appeared from his cabin. We finished the snowman, then a snowball appeared in Mike's hand. Nothing was safe from the ensuing bombardment: trees, buildings, cars, goats, each other. It was a welcome break, though the stark blankness of my inner landscape waited for my return.

Reading in my sleeping bag one evening, I wondered what to eat for dinner, then realized there was nothing to look forward to, then realized there was nothing to *ever* look forward to and nothing worth remembering. I started sinking into this nothingness, then remembered my self as a separate being, and where I was in that moment. I realized *that* particular self did not matter either, nor did the feeling of nothingness which was an experience of *that* solitary self. I broke out in laughter. Even the void had no meaning. "I am here," I thought, "with my book, and that is enough."

At last, winter made its soggy transition into spring, and snow transformed to mud. As the thaw continued, one fact became painfully clear: the outhouse would soon reach the point of overflow. A simple hole in the ground, our winter-long deposits slowly inched towards ground level. Sitting there in the dark, chill wind blowing on my ass, I saw the irony in one of Rose's comments: "Summon determination by getting angry at yourself," he said, "Sooner or later, you will see life is a bunch of crap."

A few days later, I sat outside, propping a chair in the sun on the bare, concrete slab that was an unfinished wing of the Community Building. The temperature was a balmy thirty-something. I tried to meditate, but thoughts of suicide flitted through my brain. A tiny brown bird landed, hopped towards me, then jumped onto my shoulder. Moments later, its partner landed on my head. Their life seemed so pure and simple in contrast to my cynicism that tears came to my eyes.

Though Rose was unwilling or unable to organize any group activities, he was still valuable in conversation. All I knew of my approach to seeking was one of push and attack. To "storm the gates of Heaven," was a phrase I borrowed from Rose, as if I would push my way into my mind through sheer force and tear open its secrets. There was little in my vocabulary of love or devotion. I hatched the idea of locking myself in a cabin and refusing to leave until enlightened or dead. I told this to Rose and his answer surprised me.

"I wouldn't recommend it," he said. "The determination is to be admired, but the attitude is wrong. You're challenging whatever is up there. You're saying enlightenment or death, but that may not be following the natural course. If you get help, it will be because you ask for it; not because you demand it."

What was it to ask for help? I wondered.

Chapter 7:
Goat Hugging

I asked Mr. Rose if I would ever feel I was doing everything I should. "No," he said, "and that has been the curse of my life."

The glacial misery of winter thawed and new ideas arose with the spring. A comment from Mr. Rose pointed me towards asking for help and listening, rather than fighting and pushing. "You're sensitive," he said, "but your heart is in a locked box." It was a poetic way of saying my intuition was blocked. There was no drama in the delivery of this observation. It was idly dropped like a note about the weather, and I did nothing more than record it in my notebook. It was memorable, though, because he rarely made such direct, unsolicited comments. The words percolated and found a foothold in my mind. There was still a barrier between me and others. I was still the "big stiff" at some level and that hampered my search.

A spiritual seeker in Rose's view had two tools: logic and intuition. Intuition was a mystery to me—lumped together with palm readers, psychics, mind-reading, ghost-hunting, mediums, and assorted extrasensory arts. Rose and Belle both described the intuition as refined feeling. Feelings were hard enough for me to understand in general, much less refine them. My family never discussed feelings, and I recognized only the grossest of emotions: anger, fear, happiness, sadness, contentment, and boredom. My mental machine's program was simple: avoid anger and fear, and seek happiness and contentment. The subtle currents of the inner atmosphere of emotions were virtually unknown.

Rose believed in developing the intuition like a muscle and advocated celibacy and experiments such as reading ESP cards. I practiced card reading off and on since the early days of the Zen Den, but showed no progress beyond random guessing. As for celibacy, if there was an effect it was hardly cumulative since I felt no more intuitive after a year of celibacy than after six months. Despite this handy excuse for breaking celibacy in the name of the scientific method, I had no desire for a "before and after" test. I needed additional tools, so when Belle encouraged me to try "heart-thinking" I was willing despite having no idea what she meant. Little did I know I would soon be hugging farm animals.

This might seem a distraction from looking directly for the source of thought, and backing away from untruth. I believed that to be the most direct path, but such looking increasingly brought me to an interior black wall I could not breach. That black wall was a darkness from which thoughts suddenly appeared. Perhaps that wall was self-created—a reflection a wall between me and others?

I began heart-thinking, not with hugs, but by asking what I felt at points throughout the day. While chopping a tree stump, I stopped and asked "What am I feeling right now?" Exhausted, yes, but what else? Many times I did not know. Asking that question caused an odd sensation—as if I was listening, but the "ear" was my attention turned inward rather than out. Rose once called intuition "the language of the heart," and there was definitely something faintly stirring inside, even if I had no words to translate it.

Joseph Sadony's *Gates of the Mind* offered tantalizing clues about the intuition. Sadony spoke of mental radio waves which struck the strings of our experiences. Sadony centered his life on these intuitions and became a man of refined feeling. He said if we stopped thinking and allowed feelings to be felt first, then we let the truth shape us. The feelings would get clothed by imagination born of the sum of our experiences. As a simple example, when I touched the corner of a table the first micro-impressions of that contact were pure feeling. An instant later, my mind created an image of what I was touching. It was easy to miss the feeling and only notice the thought image. Not only that, but most of my interior experience involved creating images that then caused a feeling. This stream of images fed emotional reactions that fed ever more images and imagination-caused feelings. I was shaping a "truth" born of thoughts rather than allowing the truth to shape me.

Sadony carried notebooks to record his impressions wherever he went, and vowed to always give time to notice these feelings. If he heard the voice of his feelings he would stop and listen, even in the midst of swinging a hammer. Following his example, I determined to improve my feeling capacity by whatever means imaginable.

Though the thought of it felt ridiculous (which was exactly my problem—thinking, then feeling), I hugged a tree. While no one was watching I leaned in and settled my chest and arms against the rough trunk. I turned my attention inward and looked for a feeling. There was no sudden translation of tree-speak, but it did feel like a living being rather than a brick wall. There was life or energy *out there* that I felt *in here*. I never noticed this before.

I took "heart-thinking" and applied it to meditation as well. Rather than focusing attention on my mind, I focused it on the area of my chest and heart and saw what arose. There were no distracting preconceptions because I had no idea what I was doing. Augie's admonition to "just hit something" came to mind. Take action and learn from what happens.

Like Sadony, I tried taking action whenever I felt a calling. Patching the perennially leaky trunk of my car, I felt a stirring in my heart and an odd feeling pulling me towards the woods. I easily could have ignored this and focused on the task at hand, but I put down my tools and walked until I felt like stopping. There amongst the tall poplars I asked God aloud to please let me feel him. I listened intently for an answer. Although I did not feel God, neither did I feel hopeless or alone. Once again there was something out there that I also felt inside me.

Such dramatic moments were the outlier, though. I generally felt nothing when trying to feel my heart. I looked to nature: plunging my hands in the cool waters of a stream, touching the soft moss growing at the base of a maple tree, and breathing deep the smell of bark and leaf as if trying to slide into nature's skin. Despite these diggings, I often felt only the reactions of the senses. However, even if it was just me and an empty universe, at least I was feeling.

Where did farm animals fit into this story? The Farm's goat herd was ornery and inbred, with a con-glomeration of deficient characteristics that included birthing their kids during the coldest, harshest time of the year. The few that survived the winter ran and jumped delightedly about the muddy fields of spring, and Belle suggested I play with the babies. They were not raised for petting and froze in fear when I picked them up. Holding these stiff-legged bundles, I told myself this therapy was good for both man and goat and took an interest in their little lives.

While I snuck around hugging babies and trees, Rose visited more as the weather improved. We listened for the slamming of doors like watchmen, then peered down the hill to look for his brown van. Unfortunately, Alex noted that our talks with Rose were increasingly "like putty" — vague and without direction. Was this more Zen or was it forgetfulness? I should have known something was wrong, but Rose still flashed crystal-clear one-liners:

"The more I talk, the less you listen," he said.

"Through consistent effort you become."

He commented that people in the old group expected him to "zap" them, then strikingly said, "I play a very minor role in one's becoming. You are the path; you are the way."

I took this as an acknowledgement to keep exploring the heart and forget any hopes of transmission. Though I attempted to talk with Rose about exploring the feelings inspired by nature, he conflated these with bodily emotions. "Beauty does not equate with the spiritual," he said, "neither does peace." I did not argue the point, but did not stop my experiments either. I was not chasing peace or beauty and knew such feelings were transient. What was their source, though? Did they emanate from the same place as thought?

The search for feelings spread through my life at the Farm and beyond. Both Belle and Danny recommended I find work with children. While time away from the world was valuable, Rose did not think work necessarily hindered the spiritual path. In his lecture, "Zen and Death," he described his spiritual search as a young man. He would rent a room where "no one could bother him" and get into a nightly routine of reading and meditation. Work gave him things to think about, and it proved equally so for me. Working with children especially gave me plenty to think about, such as my anger.

My close encounter with children occurred in an environmental education program for fifth graders. I quickly learned I knew nothing about teaching children. On my first day, they seemed intent on disobeying every rule I belatedly concocted. A stick was thrown; please don't throw sticks, I patiently asked. A rock was thrown; no throwing rocks, I commanded. Dirt was thrown; no throwing anything, I thundered! The line between learning, fun, and madness was entirely unclear. Kids were pushed, branches broken, and the shifty-eyed worst of them mutinied during the nature walk. I threatened and cajoled, but they were as wild as the goats. By day's end the kids did not like me, and I did not like them.

Despite my anger and frustration, my feeling repertoire broadened as the days passed. I found myself laughing on a high hill overlooking the ribbon-like curve of the Ohio River, in complete relaxation and freedom from the confines of my personality. In a timeless moment, I knelt in the woods with a group of ten year old boys, doodling in the dirt with sticks as they mused over the mystery of girls. We were suspended between the present moment and the next—only the eternal theme of opposites playing out its dance.

I learned to decipher the difference between the controlled chaos of children learning about nature, and the chaos of children reenacting *Lord of the Flies*. It was a messy, uncertain exploration that continued as I was hired for the summer day camp and repeated the environmental program for its fall season. As long as I set aside time each evening for meditation, reading, or thinking about the day, I felt progress. It was my version of Rose's nightly routine. If I got too busy, though, or spent much time talking after work, I lost hope and wanted to retreat to the Farm as everything seemed a distraction.

Stepping outside of my narrow definition of meditation and engaging with the world outside the Farm opened doors to new experiences. I sat in a large, log-framed dining hall after a long day of teaching. The hall was vintage Civilian Conservation Corps with enormous wooden beams, plank floors, and the dim corners of a vaulted ceiling darkened from the smoke of countless fires in the stone fireplace. The children had a little free time before evening activities. The dining hall's screen doors were wide open, letting in a spray of golden light from the setting sun. Inside, two girls played an upright piano. The laughter of unseen children drifted through the open doors as I reclined against a wooden table, taking it all in like a long, slow breath of air. I saw a small group laying in the grass, their feet idly keeping time to an unknown rhythm. My senses were tuned into this moment, the world around me moving in perfection. Extremely present, I paradoxically felt barely there, as if I was fading into music and light. I was momentarily swept up, released from the bonds of *self*—then in a flash I was back in my old thoughts wondering if the children liked me. Why did such moments fade?

These adventures into feeling did not eliminate my puzzling over the koan of "the view is not the viewer." Who was I if everything observed was not me? Worse yet, what did it mean when I noticed my awareness—the very awareness some claimed as the goal of searching? Danny, after weeks either in isolation or in his bunk, emerged from one of his long silences and offered an inspiring conversation. It was surprisingly rare to talk of the details of meditation with anyone, even Rose. Language being such a barrier to describing these inner experiences that any discussion quickly became a Tower of Babel. Yet with Danny, I shared a similar struggle.

Danny fought with bringing the mind back to awareness and found it exhausting. He compared the mind to a baby whose head was constantly bobbing around and attracted by everything. Danny noted how we perceived an external event, then our minds built upon it—distorting it into our own creation. We entered our heads and lost the moment. Yet, and here was the rub, the moment was in our minds as well! That conundrum drove us both to the hypothesis that if we could control our minds enough and hold them in one-pointed atten-tion, we would break through this puzzle. That the mind could outwit the mind made no logical sense, but at a gut level we believed that any problem would yield under enough focus and determination.

Danny speculated that the gap between observed and observer (the view and the viewer, and awareness of awareness) was all in our minds. Inspired, I took up the hammer of meditation again and again, concentrating on the black space or wall from which thoughts arose, as if I might break this wall through sheer focus. The only measure of progress was how many seconds I could stare before awareness drifted away. Try as I might, I never broke through.

As fall ushered in my second year on the Farm, I at last felt more like a seasoned resident than a visitor. I purchased a used chainsaw and began building the wood stockpile in early October. Rather than enjoying walks in the woods, however, my mind now catalogued dead and downed trees: how close they were to the Lodge, the quality of the wood, and how difficult to cut. Where interest lies, so goes the attention. To this day, I can't help sizing up the quality of potential firewood wherever I go.

My work with children ended for the year, but even in the stripped-down simplicity of life on the Farm distractions were everywhere. The mind looked forward to a walk, or even the one o'clock arrival of the mail. There was no fool-proof retreat from life when the simplest matter became a distraction. Yet people tried. One TAT member built an isolation chamber in his basement. It was a sound and lightproof room designed as the perfect solitary retreat. His mind, however, occupied itself with dreams and fantasies even in the utter dark and quiet. We were all the same in that respect. There was some basic untruth about the self which could not be revealed solely by retreating from the world. Though I wanted to find an answer, the mind was constantly tempted to turn away from looking.

In theory, I knew the way to enlightenment. "Back away from untruth until you reduce your sense of I-ness to the point of extinction. Reduce awareness to a point and it expands to infinity." I said that easily enough. Though these statements were logically satisfying, the reality of living them, acting upon them, or understanding them experientially escaped me. My mind created tidy packages of logic, which I crushed with the gut-level realization that "I know nothing and am full of shit." That end-of-the-day honesty was one thing I had going for me, but the same thought could carry me into depression if judged as a personal failing.

Danny emerged from a week's-long "enlightenment or bust" isolation looking busted and announced he was moving back to Raleigh. He gave enlightenment his best try, he said, and Rose was no longer of help. Alex decided to return to school in the spring and began working long hours to save money, leaving me with many evenings alone. Rose told Bob F. to leave the Farm, convinced that he was stealing. What was worth stealing was a mystery to me, as the Farm was a wasteland of junk. Once again, was it old age or Zen at the root of Rose's increasingly unexpected behavior? As the Farm quieted through attrition, my journal attested that I was fully capable of distracting myself with misery:

> There is something about the time indoors just after eating. Nothing to do but read, except I am exhausted of reading. I could meditate, but meditation gives no answers, so I could eat again, but I'm not hungry, so I lie in bed counting my breaths rather than lapsing into daydream, though I can't even count to ten without my attention drifting, so I just hate and think of lashing out at everything that moves. At least in the daydreams there is some relief. Please just take my head away and let me rest in peace. I want to sleep. I don't want peace, I want to know the truth. Won't someone split my head open and find my true self? Please help me, I am breaking under the stress. Please let me relax. Please give me an answer.

I escaped to Kentucky for Christmas, driving Belle to the airport on the way. She provided an earful of advice — suggesting that when I reached the point of "waiting" in meditation, knowing nothing else to do, that I use prayer and the heart. The heart being, in her words, "the feeling of holding a kitten you care for." She said to reach up to heaven rather than waiting for grace to descend. I listened, but despite all my attention to feeling I still had the attitude that feelings were projections—images upon a screen—and fundamentally unreal. I did not trust Sadony's contention that feelings were the root of which thoughts were a leaf-like expression. Thought seemed more real than feelings to me.

Suddenly however, it struck me for the first time that thought, too, was just as projected. I did not know if feeling was more real, but both thought and feeling were perhaps equally unreal. The only certainty was I knew nothing for certain. On top of that uncertainty, Rose's increasing forgetfulness, and the slow departure of our tiny community left me wondering if I would be the last man standing.

Chapter 8:
I Will Take Leave of Thee

*Tenacity of purpose and honesty in pursuit
will bring you to your goal.*

—*Nisargadatta Maharaj*

In our best moments, Alex and I studied and meditated during the day, then shared stories around the wood stove as night fell, waves of heat warming chilled hands. Orange peels placed on top of the stove slowly charred, filling the Lodge with a pleasant smell of citrus. Our thoughts twisted and played with one another and yielded inspirations. It was much like Rose wrote:

> I have always estimated play as a happy ingredient of efficiency. It is a known fact that the subconscious mind gives forth its inspirations under a lassitude of the conscious. By this I seem to discredit concentration.

Concentration is not a strained method of forcing the mind upon a certain train of thought. We can best study a proposition when we are interested in it. And interest means ease. It is a harmonious corresponding of the mind, – either by memory, or reason with environment. This reacting with environment is accomplished in reading, holding conversation, or by any other method which arouses the memory. The result of interest is frequently inspiration, which is often a sudden illumination of the memory, or the arriving congruency of two past memories hitherto unrelated.

A winter to read and think about whatever I wanted should have felt a blessing. Yet this winter, frustration with my spiritual path again leaked into my interactions with those around me. Alex's long hours at work meant his occasional presence seemed like the crinkling of plastic in a quiet room. I dwelled on minutiae like the sound of his pencil scratching on his notebook. I saw myself getting angry and obsessed on my reactions to these situations—lamenting my silent criticism. Why couldn't I have thoughts of understanding rather than judgment? An endless round of mentally flogging others, then flogging myself for the flogging ensued. To escape, I fled to the tumbledown green trailer that was Bob's former abode. Lopsided, the trailer was falling to its knees, slowly sinking into the earth like a wounded animal. Despite its decrepitude, the emptiness was a temporary savior.

Belle's advice about prayer and kittens was good, but slipped from my mind as the heavy grey of winter overwhelmed my efforts to unlock the box around my heart. Bitter cold and isolation drove me toward more watching of thoughts. I sat for hours on a wooden chair, nursing the trailer's tiny wood stove and trying to meditate. There was all the time in the world to study my mind, but I could not force myself to use it fully. At best, I puzzled over the illogical belief that thoughts *about* thinking which occurred outside of meditation were "mine." I in some way controlled those thoughts unlike the ones I observed in meditation. Logically, all thoughts fit into one bucket called "thought," yet experientially I claimed and identified with some, but not others.

I honed in on the feeling of "I-ness," that tangible, wordless sense that I existed and was an independent entity. I grasped for the feeling of the opposite of I-ness: the sense of nonexistence. What will "I" be when I no longer exist? What would it feel like to not exist? That was as personal and practical as a koan could be, yet just as daunting to the logical mind as the traditional Zen koan "Does the dog have a Buddha nature?"

My anger at these unsolvable questions mounted. Despite Mr. Rose's warning against challenging the forces that be, I faced-off with an unknown God only to get swatted down again and again. "I won't leave this chair till my question is answered!" I swore, yet within ten minutes that determination evaporated. The depth of unknowing was astonishing, and it was increasingly obvious that on a minute-to-minute basis I had no idea which of the many "I's" was in control.

Never one to let a dead horse go unbeaten, I revisited the tool of Vipassana meditation. I sat in that wooden chair naming each object that appeared in consciousness, impassively objectifying thoughts and sensations as they streamed out from their hidden source. Only now my mind trapped itself by naming the process of naming: I saw thoughts, named them, then saw myself naming them and named that process "naming." This tail chasing became a mental dead end. What was beyond naming the naming? I knew nothing else to do, however, and my meditation practice ground on through the winter.

Interrupting this grind, the annual goat birthing began as the weather turned to its worst. With everyone away except Alex and me, I became the chief goat herder. Feeding and watering was the extent of my goat husbandry, so I was as clueless as a first-time mother when babies arrived. I naively thought nature would take a happy course. Instead, the barn descended into tragedy: one goat refused to feed its kid, another kid froze to death during the night, then an adult froze the next day. I had no idea what to do. The same powerlessness that kept me using the hopelessly dull "Zen saw" my first winter, now kept me from doing anything more than witnessing the death accumulating around me. Like a child, I expected someone else to come to the rescue.

The ground was too hard to bury the dead, so I loaded the bodies into the garden wagon. The cold of its metal handle bit into my glove as I dragged the wagon through the snow and towards a ridge line. Breathing heavily, the bandana covering my face became stiff as the moisture froze. At the edge of the ridge, I tossed the stiffened bodies as far as I could. They were heavy, and the snow and trees kept them from sliding out of view. "How did my life come to this?" I asked. "What kind of spiritual quest is this?" The next morning, I found another adult dead in its stall.

Anger finally roused Alex and me from this stupor of helplessness. Two more babies were plaintively crying—a wobbly wail we recognized as a death sign. We scooped them up and took them to the Lodge, but they would not eat. Panic and despair roiled inside me. In a flash of inspiration, I remembered Art telling how he rattled dried corn in an old coffee can and the goats would come running to the sound. I grabbed a few kernels and rattled them in an empty can. The babies stumbled excitedly towards me and ate a few kernels! We repeated this process over the next several hours as they teetered between this world and death—the rattling of dried corn pulling them from the brink each time. We built a makeshift pen under my desk and lived with the sounds and smells of baby goats for several days, until they were strong enough and the worst of the cold receded.

As the cold passed, so did the last of our community. Alex left for Raleigh at the end of March, Mike C. moved a couple of hours away to Columbus, and Art left his bat-ridden trailer for a house in town—telling me he had given up hope. As quickly as our little group rose up, now it was gone. Rose was the thread that bound us, and now that fabric was tearing. There was no more talk of rapport sittings, and when Rose did come to the Farm it was from suspicion of thievery or some other imagined problem.

Realizing the need to keep motivated, I offered to help one of the old-timers start a group in Pittsburgh. Rose saw working with fellow seekers as key to progress and called this the "Law of the Ladder." Imagine climbing up a ladder of progress. Those above you pull you up, and likewise you reach down to those below you. The people below also give you a little push up. Ideally, the ashram provided the matrix for group work, but not if there was just one guy and a herd of goats.

As the ashram faded along with Mr. Rose, I rationalized his decline as memory trouble mixed with paradoxical Zen mastery. At Belle's suggestion however, I read *The 36-Hour Day*, a guide to caring for people with memory loss. Rose's behavior was well described in the book and it wiped away my months-long denial. I will never know how much of his puzzling actions were Zen and how much were illness, but now I saw a failing brain warping every part of his life. Even the way Rose described his enlightenment experience had changed. He no longer spoke of falling into an abyss of nothingness in which the mind dissolved. Instead, he only told the beginning of the event where he was sitting in bed when an intense pain struck his head and he travelled out of his body, finding himself looking down on humanity from atop a mountain.[2] What did it mean when an enlightened man forgot his enlightenment? Was enlightenment a figment of the imagination? I eventually realized that enlightenment did not make the body immune to disease or accident. The memory of the event and even the experience of the event occurred through a physical brain. That brain was a conduit between this world and some other. Damage that conduit, and you damage the connection.

Though still helpful to visit Rose, I found myself translating our increasingly cryptic conversations. When I revealed plans to start a group in Pittsburgh, Rose told me groups were a distraction, yet when I asked him if I should help those who were not as far along as me, he said yes.

Trying to make sense of the contradiction, I said, "You seem to be saying one needs a group, but a group is a distraction."

"Well," he replied, "if twenty-five people go in silence to the chapel for the purpose of getting away from themselves, then that's good."

---

2   See http://www.searchwithin.org/download/realization_rich-ard_rose.pdf for a collection of Rose's descriptions about his experience.

I pondered the meaning of this for more than a few minutes.

Even without Rose, miracles occurred. One evening in the Lodge after a particularly stressful day, the thought of my death arose. I felt joy rather than fear. Picturing Belle, tears rolled down my face. Overtaken with a swelling, pulsing vibration through my body, joy filled my mind; love filled my heart. My heart! Undeniably I felt my heart, and ecstatic energy poured forth from it. The waves of joy and happiness eventually receded, leaving a warmth in my chest as evidence of their passing. The next day not a trace remained. I did not know what to make of it, but following Rose's advice I gave thanks and did not chase the feeling. It was a gift.

As Rose withered I took steps to find my own inspiration rather than rely on him. I attended a Near Death Experience (NDE) conference and meet nearly a dozen people with extraordinary stories of tunnels of light and love, and other mystical/psychic events. Though skeptical, I was overjoyed to meet people rather than read books. The sharp contrast between a TAT meeting where we talked of ideas, and these meetings where people talked of experiences, was welcome. Danny, in fact, made the suggestion at our last TAT meeting that we should share our successes, failures and interests, rather than talking in abstractions or waiting for Rose to ignite a conversation. The TAT group did not know how to function without Mr. Rose as the catalyst.

Meeting people and attending talks provided fuel to keep my mind active, but once again I felt I was running from the real problem. Why couldn't I simply sit and face my self in silence? That seemed the most direct path, but was so difficult. I stared at my mind until only my sense of I-ness was left. Every other thought or feeling I saw as clearly not "me." I found no place, however, from which to examine the sense of individual existence and see what lay behind it. Like a shadow, wherever I went, there *I* was.

The gifts that arose outside of my carefully planned spiritual life, spontaneous and unexpected, ever exceeded my intense efforts, but I do not think they would have occurred in absence of my striving and straining. Half asleep during the early night, I felt my chest caving in upon itself as if falling into darkness and my mind was suddenly gripped by the feeling of extinction. I let out a guttural, halting yell of protest and came fully awake in the dark—the Lodge interior dimly glowing in the light of a half-moon. The feeling vanished as swiftly as it arose. Though my instinctual reaction was fear, I immediately wished for this experience to happen again. It was an opportunity to walk though or at least stand at the doorway of death.

This lost opportunity reminded me of H.G. Wells' short story "The Door in the Wall." In it, Lionel Wallace was haunted by an experience as a young child where he walked through a mysterious green door and discovered a wonderful garden.

There was something in the very air of it that exhilarated, that gave one a sense of lightness and good happening and well-being; there was something in the sight of it that made all its colour clean and perfect and subtly luminous. In the instant of coming into it one was exquisitely glad—as only in rare moments, and when one is young and joyful one can be glad in this world. And everything was beautiful there...
And it was like coming home.

After many wondrous experiences in the garden, Wallace found himself transported back to the dull streets of London with the green door nowhere in sight. Through the years, he glimpsed the green door again, but each time chose to ignore it for more pressing matters of commonplace life. His regrets built till, weary with the world and longing for the doorway, he lamented:

Thrice I have had my chance—THRICE! If ever that door offers itself to me again, I swore, I will go in out of this dust and heat, out of this dry glitter of vanity, out of these toilsome futilities. I will go and never return. This time I will stay... I swore it and when the time came—I DIDN'T GO.

I prayed I did not do the same. I sensed the feeling of extinction was a doorway that led to freedom, if only I would face the fear. Such moments lent hope that I was on the right track.

As Rose felt less well, I spent more time around the farmhouse cutting grass or weeding the garden, and getting glimpses of Rose outside of his teaching role. One astonishing evening, I found the Zen master reclining on the couch watching the television comedy *Married With Children*. "There's not much on TV I can stand," he said, "but that Bundy [the long-suffering husband], I like him." Ironically, as Rose became less the teacher, I felt more comfortable around him. Driving him on an errand, Rose recited a history of the neighboring properties. "There," he pointed, "was a blacksmith's shop on that corner." We approached a curve with a dirt lane leading into the woods. "That road led to my back farm, before the Krishnites leased it. When it rained, you couldn't get a vehicle back there and it was a two mile walk to the house." I was co-pilot to a time traveler and felt a great warmth towards this old man. There were no koans, no parables, and no stories to twist into commentary on my personality. We simply shared a ride—he, the wise grandfather I never knew.

Even in his decline, people looked to Rose for help. One night I listened as Rose patiently answered a phone call. Later, he told me the caller was "spiritually attacked." "Sometimes you just start crying, and you don't know why," Rose said. "The attack opens your head, and you gain new understanding once it is over. The thing to do is go off by yourself and wait it out, knowing that it will end. People around you will think you are going crazy, so best to be alone."

In baby steps, I drew away from the Farm. The first day of the July TAT meeting, I left early in the morning and went to a NDE meeting instead. This was the first TAT meeting I missed since moving to West Virginia. Returning late in the evening, I did not regret my TAT mutiny. People sat around and small talked while waiting for Rose to start the discussion. He never did.

In one of his poems, Rose presciently wrote,

I will take leave of you
Not by distinct farewell
But vaguely
As one entering vagueness
For words, symbols of confusion
Would only increase confusion
But silence, seeming to be vagueness,
Shall be my cadence,
Which someday
You will understand.

I felt this happening, as if Rose less and less poked his head out from the silence engulfing him. We had a short, but inspiring talk mid-summer. "People are taught from an early age that you have to 'take it.' I don't have to take anything," he said, "All I have to do is die."

This statement was particularly confrontational for an introvert like me who was inclined to shrug and do as he was told. "That's just the way it is and you might as well get used to it," a friend said in my undergrad days. I did not like his words, but had no rebuttal. Rose's statement was a rebuttal etched into the blade of a hatchet.

This night, Rose was in a rare mood and lucid, so I shared how I got inspired and thought I was close to an answer, but then fell short.

"I know," he softly said with a feeling of compassion that surprised me.

"This is important," he said, his voice rising in tone. "You have to accept what comes. You should say to yourself verbally what you want, but accept what comes."

Such lessons I hoped to remember.

Rose also said, "Life will be the teacher." One long, sweaty, fly-bitten afternoon, after seeming hours trying to remove the oil filter on Belle's car, I flung my tools in disgust. My filter wrench was slightly too large in diameter and kept sliding off. It was impossible to finish with the tools at hand. I launched into a tirade about this being emblematic of all the problems on the Farm. "Mr. Rose would get this filter off," I said, "even if he had to build his own wrench and it took two weeks. Well, he's wrong. It is not worth the time spent. You could pay someone to do this with two hours of your salary!"

"Yeah, you're right," Belle said, then paused, "…how about a rock?"

Her suggestion halted my tirade. Picking up a small piece of gravel, I wedged it between the edge of the filter and the wrench and… it worked.

My outrage and argument with the world collapsed. There were no excuses, no criticizing her advice, or "yeah, but" rationalizations. I saw and admitted to her that I was completely wrong. My fuming arguments and damning pronouncements were based on a misperception. It was a remarkably odd feeling, like a weight lifted. To admit being wrong was freeing rather than defeating. The truth really did set me free.

Despite these small realizations, I needed a change. I spent a few weeks in Raleigh in hopes that a deep dive into civilization might unearth a new spiritual direction for me, or even a role in the larger-than-ever SKS. Flourishing and filled with enthusiastic camaraderie, there was still what Doug called the "Donuts for Enlightenment" mentality—where the hustle and bustle of fundraising, group events, and marketing was considered spiritual work in and of itself. I thought I could always go back to the SKS, but finally realized this meant resuming a role in which I no longer believed. By year's end, Rose was completely out of the picture. His mind lost in the fog of what we assumed was Alzheimer's. As for me, I was stuck between Raleigh and the Farm, both seeming like stagnation.

Chapter 9:
Winter, Summer, Winter

Sad twilight cricket,
once again I have wasted those daylight hours.

—Rikei

As my third winter on the Farm began, Belle became my confidant and advisor filling some of the void of Rose's decline. She had a job in town, but often stayed at the farmhouse despite the freezing cold and sometimes brought Mr. Rose along to give his wife a respite. If Belle was alone, I came down the hill to light the wood stove. The house was near freezing and she would stand there, bundled in an enormous quilted coat, chatting with me until the room warmed enough to sit down. We had more time together, but our relationship was even more abstracted from any thought of romance. Belle suggested we stop hugging and even the playful voices we used when feeling close to one another. "When we touch, our bodies are awake, but our minds are asleep," she said. I agreed to this, but only after she wooed my stomach with her home-made biscuits. In private, I wept for the feeling of comfort and home that holding Belle brought to me, though I suspected it was what Rose called "the beauty of illusion."

Once again, whatever progress I made during the warmer months to cultivate my heart-feeling dissipated with the cold. For a few days, I tried a half-hearted discipline of prayer, but never mustered any sincerity. The only prayer I occasionally uttered with conviction was, "Please let me find an answer." That simple lament was true, but went unfulfilled. Despite my efforts to cultivate intuition, I still did not believe that was the most direct path. Intuition, prayer, feeling, and heart; all seemed faint, meandering paths to who-knows-where. The surest way was to look at my mind with my mind.

With no one left on the Farm to dissuade me, I undertook a week-long retreat dubbed the "isolation of desperation." I sat in Bob's green trailer and intended to meditate as much as possible. I soon discovered the mind had other ideas. Hour after hour my mind drifted, and the only discipline I maintained was counting to ten over and over. There was no strength of mind, no focus, and no desire. It was painfully obvious that I regularly observed the processes of my mind (the "Process Observer" Rose referred to in his *Psychology of the Observer*), but my experience stopped there. Just as I felt stuck on the Farm, I was stuck in meditation. Awareness was unable to see behind itself.

I studied Rose's words in the *Psychology of the Observer* hoping for a light to dawn. My mind wandered to the memory of discussing this book on the SKS van ride to the Farm years ago. Puzzling over this thin book was nothing new as it was the closest Rose came to formulating a map of the stages leading to enlightenment. Rose said every point of being (or perspective) had a polar point until one reached an absolute experience. The polar point to my Process Observer was unknown to me. I saw the judgments of the lower mind that Rose called the "Umpire," labelling pleasure and pain, right and wrong, and good and bad. I saw, as well, the logic and intuition witnessed by the Process Observer. The mind built logical steps to its conclusions, and the mind received feelings which influenced my actions. I observed both the logic-building of thought and the receiving of feeling.

However, in his diagram called "Jacobs Ladder" Rose labelled an opposite point to the Process Observer which he called the "Individual Consciousness of Awareness."[3] These words meant nothing to me, and I vaguely imagined this Consciousness as some kind of super-intuitive sense beyond that familiar to me. I recognized the foolishness of parsing his words and thinking I could intellectually accept or refute his map. The only way to know was to go *there* and see—all the while remembering that what I could see and observe was not me.

---

3   Image reprinted by permission of Cecy Rose at RichardRose-Teachings.com.

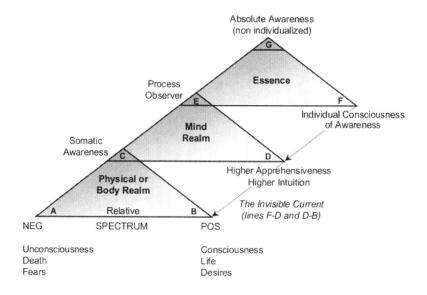

But no seeing was happening. By the end of the week in the trailer, I literally could no longer look inside my self. When I sat to meditate, my body and mind involuntarily recoiled. It was shockingly similar to a long ago experience of eating a half dozen donuts, then being offered another one. "No!" was the response from both the mind and gut. Even the *thought* of meditation made my head woozy. My hammer of meditation was broken.

With meditation practice in shambles, the one clear fact of my spiritual search was that I would die, and I had no idea what death meant. Everything I knew was an assumption, and the thought of death turned my head back to the search despite the apparent futility of searching. Death became my motivator of last resort, and I was increasingly at last resorts.

Fortuitously, I had picked up Sherwin Nuland's *How We Die* on my trip to Raleigh. Dr. Nuland's masterful storytelling coupled the cold clinical facts of suicide, AIDS, cancer, accidents, euthanasia, murder, Alzheimer's and heart attacks, with a vignette from the life of a victim of each. He shattered the myth of the "good death," wherein my last moments would see me stoically contemplating my impending demise, reading Zen koans, and meditating. Odds were, I'd die with a tube in my mouth and stupefied from painkillers. I read these stories, then sat quietly as my problems subsided before the looming shadow of death. Dying vicariously, in this quiet space I wavered at the edge of feeling my extinction, but did not fall over that edge. This was the only practice I had left—an intuitive sense that if I tarried with these feelings then the truth of who I was might hit me.

Winter rolled into spring with moments of inspiration coming at the strangest times. Rose was always interested in the supernatural and had a lifetime of strange encounters he loved to share. There were tales of ghostly heads floating in the upstairs hallway, and shadowy entities hovering behind people who mixed sex and drugs. There was his dead brother James who visited him in such life-like dreams that Rose became sleep-deprived from their intensity. Or his dead brother Joe who told Rose how glad he was to be free of his body. While I could shrug off these stories in the light of day, night lent them a peculiar potential for reality. After a hefty dose of such tales, Rose would bid me goodnight and send me into the gloom to walk up the hill to the Lodge. Rather than admiring the clarity of the stars, I stared at every shadow, looking for demons and spirits, then worriedly glanced over my shoulder for the ghastly *thing* that surely followed me.

Remembering these tales, one night in early spring, I walked up that hill with two visitors from Raleigh. We walked in silence. There were no monsters, only stars overhead and the sharp crunch of our feet on the gravel. I felt us linked, players in a play, moving in unison as if made to journey up this particular hill in that very moment. I stretched out my arms and the night flowed through the shell I called my self. I was defenseless and opened my self to whatever was present. Everything was perfect.

These glimpses helped shake off the chain of anger, frustration, and depression I felt around my heart, but I still felt I needed more. I looked for a replacement for Mr. Rose even though I knew no one could give me enlightenment. In Pittsburgh there was Jim Burns, a chain smoking schizophrenic prone to falling into verbal rants about beating God with a baseball bat. Rose had met him years ago and thought him enlightened. Belle found Jim incredibly helpful, but I failed to find inspiration in his teachings. Looking further afield, at Danny's suggestion I journeyed to the University of Science and Philosophy at Swannanoa, Virginia. Once home to Walter Russell, "the man who tapped the secrets of the universe," I found an enormous but faded mansion where a handful of his students gathered to preserve Russell's legacy. These caretakers could only *talk* about Russell's philosophy, though. No one had the real experience of it. I hoped this was not the future of TAT...

I got another dose of death from the movie *Threads*—a sobering portrayal of the unraveling of civilization after a nuclear attack. Watching it alone in the basement of a friend's office, the pointlessness of the struggle to live overtook me. Weeping, I felt an impulse to read Rose's poem "The Dawn Breaks."[4]

> The dawn breaks because another day and
> night have died,
> But the sky was there through all.
> The butterfly floats a moment and then
> his dalliance is only an eternal picture.
> The breast flows with milk and is dry forever.
> And the lullaby of life and the ear
> that hear it weaken and cease.
>
> Nothing is happening. Nothing is done.
> The sun rises in glory and the lover
> stretches his shoulders with ambition,
> The sunset is forever, and the lover
> drinks of beauty,
> And beauty drinks of the lover
> And life loses its pride in death.

---

4   Reprinted by permission of Cecy Rose at RichardRoseTeachings.com, from *Carillon* by Richard Rose.

But nothing is happening. Nothing is done.
The eye and the urge are beauty and life,
The owner is disenfranchised
The holder lets go his grasp and everything
becomes his domain.
God is in his thought, and his thought lives
only in his God.
Nothing is judged. Nothing is known.
Nothing is meaningful. Everything is perfect.

The loss contained in the thought of letting go was nearly overwhelming. "Take me," I asked and begged with all my heart to whatever was listening. My mind wavered on an edge where in front of me was all I knew and behind me was the unknown. I did not fall backwards into that unknown. Instead, the weeping subsided. Still standing, I could not see how to push myself off this cliff. Some teachers preached "Just let go," but if I could have, I would. Was a fickle act of grace the only way to back away from the last untruth?

I wanted to ask Rose, but the Zen master's mind was lost. I sat with him one afternoon, keeping an eye while his wife was away. He puttered in the kitchen as if looking for something, then finally settled down when I offered a cup of coffee. "Mr. Rose," I asked, "do you know what will happen to you when you die?"

"Yeah," he said, in a gravelly whisper that sent chills down my spine. His next words, though, were an indecipherable salad.

My obsession with death subsided as the weeks passed, like many inspirations before it. That quality of the mind—to get excited, plateau, then fade—wasn't to be lamented. It's just how the mechanism worked. Seeing that time and again helped me to eventually avoid the depressions that arose as inspiration faded, but this took years.

Later in summer, I returned to Kentucky to visit family and received an unexpected lesson from my uncle. Unlike my late father, Terry was a risk-taker, having been a magazine publisher, real estate broker, and full-time gambler. We sat with a glass of iced tea as he asked what I was doing in the West Virginia woods. I knew he liked Thoreau, so I used that to segue into wondering what life was all about. He nodded in agreement, then shared some thoughts from his "wonderings."

"When you have a worry," Terry said, "think about how you're going to handle it, then forget about it." This was strikingly familiar to Rose's advice to set your mind to do something, then forget about it.

Terry also explained, "I think everything is a circle. It all goes back to what it was, and I think everything is related. If you could go back millions of years and find out what that rock was before it was a rock, you might know what everything is."

"It's all a matter of perspective. You've got to find a table to stand on to get the perspective. How the hell do you find the table?" he said, laughing and shaking his head.

Still hunting for my own version of that table, I
traveled to Florida to investigate Dr. Shantung Zuber
III, author of the impressively titled *The Underlying Roots
of Consciousness.* A fortuitous friendship provided me a
multi-million dollar duplex on the beach just minutes
from Shantung's address. It was sitting empty and in need
of a house-sitter. I took this as a sign that I was destined
to meet Shantung, discover the next guru, and lead the
children of TAT to their new home.

I called Shantung's office repeatedly to speak with
him about his book, but he was never available. Finally,
his assistant told me to make a paid appointment with
him for chi adjustments. She relayed a message from
Shantung that his book was for enlightenment of the
mind, and he was now interested in enlightenment of the
body. The thought of paying to talk to someone about
their book was so astounding that I assumed his assistant
had not passed on my messages. If Shantung understood
the sincerity of my quest, surely he would talk with me.

I soon found out the truth, as I happened upon
an advertisement for a public talk by my elusive target.
Gathered with twenty others in a small bookshop, my first
glimpse of Shantung was as if he stepped off the cover of a
romance novel—long locks of hair and deep tan set off by
a billowing white shirt. True to his assistant's message, his
entire talk focused on the body's health and well-being,
and culminated with a demonstration of Shantung's
"iron shirt." He dramatically took off his shirt, placed a

machete against his bare chest, and whacked the edge of the machete with a wooden stick. Though it left a red line on his chest, the blade didn't break the skin, proving… something… at least in Shantung's mind.

The talk concluded and I cut a path to the good doctor. The moment I said my name his face darkened. He truly had no interest in talking about enlightenment, and brusquely told me he had several enlightenment experiences and knew practices that led to enlightenment, but it was not all that important. The moment someone asked him about scheduling an appointment, he turned from me and never looked back. The great spiritual hope of Shantung proved a grand disappointment.

Belle called soon thereafter and further crushed my mood. She wanted to leave me, get married, and have children. This was too much to bear, and my mind scrambled to avert the pain. I told her I loved her, though I had avoided using the L-word for years. I felt I didn't know what love really meant, and until I did I refused to say it. Until now. I even said I would marry her, but drew the line at children. I had no conception how children fit into the path I modeled after Rose's, and having a child seemed the antithesis of his call to focus my energy towards a single purpose. Though I was grasping and still afraid to face the world alone, I would not commit seeming spiritual suicide.

We had a series of alternately gut-wrenching and inspiring talks over the next days. Belle read my journals and realized how much help she had been, and I noted my failure to share this simple fact. She stopped mentioning marriage and children, and I did not bring up the subject. For a while, we settled back into a familiar rhythm of conversation and I was content with that, though I realized she might not be.

I returned to the Farm and found my books covered with mold from the late summer's humidity—a fitting metaphor for the state of my spiritual search. It was time to go, somewhere, anywhere.

About an hour north of the Farm was an outdoor education center that provided free training, housing, and meals. I applied for work and they were happy to hire me, but the job did not start until the following spring. Despite experiencing three winters of misery, the trio of inertia, fear, and worry about money kept me pinned to the Farm for a fourth. I don't know why I expected a fourth winter would be any different. Avoiding complete insanity, I at least moved from the Lodge to the relatively luxurious cabin where Augie confronted me four and a half years prior. No more wood stove for me! Instead, electric heat, ample lighting, and a couch awaited. All the accoutrements of high living… except plumbing. I was still relegated to freezing my ass in the outhouse.

Before the snows came, Belle and I visited Danny at his new home in Virginia. There he built a small cabin on a piece of land, hidden from the road and bordering a small river. It was an idyllic retreat. Danny made a good living

selling land and was inspired once again by the search
for enlightenment. He introduced us to a guitar-playing
friend, who provided a quick lesson in music and life:

> You have to practice at least two hours every
> day if you want to be good. Me, I can't do it
> anymore. When you have a family your priori-
> ties change. Some guys would lock themselves
> in a room for eight hours a day; they made it
> like a job. When they came out, they'd have
> something great.

It was the gospel of Augie and Rose: the application
of energy led to success, and the more energy applied the
sooner that success arrived.

Inspired by this truth, I sought to lock myself in the
cabin for my last winter on the Farm and emerge with
something great. While a change of place sometimes
brought new thoughts, instead I plunged further into
hopelessness. I no longer had a meditation practice and
could not force my self to look inside. What was I to do?

With no sense of inner guidance, I opened a Tarot
deck that I found in the cabin. Reading the instructions,
a reduced draw of the Major Arcana was supposed to
provide clues about major life events. Sounded good to
me. I shuffled the deck and drew the Pope, Lover, Chariot,
Hermit, and Wheel of Fortune. The draw order pointed
to a great triumph and light shed on an obscure matter.

There was betrayal and infidelity presaged, as well. It sounded quite dramatic, but not the guidance I hoped for.

Incredibly, the next day Belle confessed she was attracted to someone else. Though she still wanted our relationship to work, she pushed me to take the lead. I did not understand what this meant, or where we were going. Only later did I realize this was precisely the problem. As for the prediction of a great triumph, I stumbled through the rest of the winter like a man on life support. There was desire to quit the spiritual search, but no replacement desire lighting a way forward. Every practice was as dull and uninspiring as sand.

Towards the end of winter, Belle, Danny, and I flew to a Bernadette Roberts retreat in California. Bernadette was in her sixties, at turns irreverent and opinionated, and a long student of Catholic mysticism. She knew the Christian spiritual journey, and her spiritual life was solidly set by age twenty-six when she attained the Unitive state — which she described as her self becoming centered in God. By her own admission Bernadette was "very limited, very narrow." Most of her retreat was so buried in the terminology of Christian mysticism that I was ready to leave by the first day. Nor did she have patience for anyone working outside of a religious framework. She advised us to join a religion because it offered more resources than a lone spiritual teacher. I felt no resonance with this advice, but shortly afterwards she made a telling remark about introverts and extroverts.

"All the mystics have been extroverts, big ones," she said. "Introverts should not be in monasteries. They have some supernatural experiences and they just fade away. They should be in the world."

Feeling the truth in this comment, I relaxed in her presence. I told her my spiritual path felt like pushing an enormous ball up a never-ending hill. Bernadette replied that I was in a rut and should do the opposite of what I was doing. This was not new advice, but hearing it from a stranger reaffirmed my decision to leave the Farm.

In my last weeks at the Farm, Belle waffled between ending our relationship and hoping I could change into the man she needed. Yet I felt the assertive man she wanted me to become betrayed my spiritual values. I knew no way to be assertive and strong except to exercise my will power and reinforce the ego. My models of "strong" men were assholes, and I interpreted this quality as adding to the ego rather than backing away from untruth. I wanted us to continue on as we always had, but knew that could not be. Amid much crying over her conviction that she must leave, a profound acceptance washed over me. I clung to the hope we would stay together, but above all I wished us spiritual fulfillment. I had no idea how resilient our connection would prove.

In mid-March, I packed my books, clothes, and sleeping bag, leaving to start work at the Linsly Outdoor Center (LOC). It was cold and damp, the ground a wet sponge, and a biting wind funneled down the lane as I trudged to my car. I had squeezed every ounce of possibility from the Farm, beaten on every door it offered, and now it was time to go. Though I was nervous about the future and this moment seemed as frigid and harsh as the air, my life on the Farm was finally passed.

Chapter 10:
Into the World

Life will be your teacher.

— Richard Rose

Though not physically far removed, my post-Farm destination was as much a world unto itself as the Farm had been. The Linsly Outdoor Center was an hour north of Wheeling, but in Pennsylvania rather than West Virginia. There, the dismal valley that hemmed in Wheeling opened into gently rolling hills that reminded me of Kentucky. Students from Pittsburgh and surrounding schools came for environmental education, plus something called "teambuilding" about which I was clueless. A former juvenile detention center, LOC consisted of a squat, cinderblock building for offices and staff housing, and two dormitories for students. It was a tiny footprint of cleared land within the 7,500 acres of Raccoon Creek State Park.

Along with five other staff members, I underwent two weeks of intensive training which began with a day of teambuilding activities. I should have known something was amiss when I showed up in an old sweatshirt and running shoes while everyone else looked like they'd fallen out of an adventure gear catalog. The grass, and shortly my shoes, were sodden with dew as I slogged through the chill morning air and into the surrounding line of oaks and maples. This was the low ropes course, which consisted of steel cables as thick as my finger bolted through trees, various dangling ropes, and low wooden platforms—imagine a children's playground engineered for football players. LOC's director squeezed us onto one of these narrow platforms and pointed to a log laying half buried in the ground twenty feet away. Between us and the log was a rope hanging from the trees. Grinning, the director looked at me and said, "Shawn, get your whole team across this pit of lava. You can't jump. Good luck."

The rope was easily ten feet away, so after the thoughts of "reach for it" and "jump for it," the brain had exhausted its creativity. "They've given us an impossible task," I silently reasoned, "just to see how we react." While I was resorting to excuses, though, my teammates were waiting for a solution. I had nothing. "I have a belt," someone said. All eyes shifted from me to the belt. "So what?" I thought to myself, "What good will that do?" Someone else offered a jacket, then a sweatshirt. The solution slowly dawned on me as I watched these bits of clothing tied to form a chain long enough to swing out and hook the rope. Rope in hand, we swung one by one across the lava pit.

The solution was all around me, but I could not see it. I felt like an idiot.

As training proceeded, my journal noted a running commentary on my failings. I struggled to tie knots with unfamiliar names: the retraced figure eight, the bowline on a bight, and the square knot. I got lost on the orienteering course. On the high ropes—similar to the low ropes, but with the cables thirty-five feet in the air—I felt like an idiot, again, and added "feeling like a scared baby" to my list of failings. Secured by a climbing rope, I inched up an enormous oak tree. Clutching the tree like a sloth, I stared at a wooden beam almost as wide as my shoe which dangled by ropes from a cable. My task was to step onto this beam, then cross a four foot gap to another beam. The beam swayed violently left and right as I gingerly placed a foot on it. Knees buckling, heart pounding, I held tight to the ropes and stepped fully onto the beam. It settled just enough for me to dare lifting a foot, then whipped left and right just as violently as before. A belayer on the ground had the end of my climbing rope and shouted encouragement. "You can do it! Just take one more step. Come on!"

Words tumbled in my mind: "I can't do it. I'm a failure. I suck. What am I doing here? I need to leave…" The more my mind raced, the more my arms lost strength and my determination faltered. I made a half-hearted attempt to take another step forward.

"I'm done. Let me down," I said.

Lowered to the ground, defeated, my SKS "never give up" attitude stared me in the face. Likewise, my meditative observations that I was not my body or my mind proved useless in overcoming the practical fears faced high in the trees. Whatever observer I thought I was found itself swept away by fear and totally identified as the body.

Despite my damning self-judgments, no one told me to pack my bags. All the staff were patient, encouraging, and helpful. Yet when evening came, I retreated to my room rather than socialize. The rest of the staff enjoyed watching movies, playing cards, listening to music, drinking, sports, and all the normal activities I had mostly avoided since meeting the SKS group. Such was my isolation that I had completely missed the 1994 Winter Olympics—I had no idea they happened. I saw this rejection of social expectations as both conserving energy and time for the spiritual search and as a subtraction of illusory norms. Despite my professed sweeping rejections, I began to enjoy this sandal-wearing collection of outdoor gear-heads.

I gravitated towards Dave, a burly, hyperactive, pot-smoking ex-infantryman from Vermont who was practically my polar opposite. Accompanying him on a three-hour romp through the woods, we jumped creeks, clambered across logs, and ended ankle-deep in the mud of a beaver pond that opened into a small valley. We stopped as if stumbling upon a wall of silence. Silence permeated the valley with that familiar edge where just *over there*, as close as my skin, something else existed. The angling light silhouetted the trees and hills, bringing their presence into bold relief. In front of us, a single duck cut through the mirror-like surface of the pond, its undulating wake rolling back into the stillness from which it arose… perhaps from which I arose? This was thread to the truth, a feeling of returning to a place half-known or forgotten, a feeling offered by that ever-present Zen master called Life. Hill, water, ripple, self—all floated in something grander, yet each was a part of that magnificence. I was completely care-free and at peace. Feeling I could stand there forever, I lingered, until the thought of walking home in the dark broke the reverie.

Bit by bit I found my way out of negativity. Collapsed in bed one night, I dreamt of a teacher drawing two points in the sand, then connecting them by closely spaced boot prints. I immediately grasped the hopeful message that putting one foot in front of the other would slowly close the gap between where I was and where I wanted to be.

Eventually I learned to tie knots, belay a climber, and teach a host of problem-solving activities like the lava pit. More than school, the SKS, or my time at the Farm, LOC taught me to think creatively and use what was at hand to solve a problem. I also found a place amongst its social structure. Despite spending my free time reading or journaling, people found me friendly and reliable… and liked my fondness for baking. Despite the protests of the kitchen manager, we were allowed all the food we could eat, and the freezer included ready-to-bake chocolate chip cookies. I hovered near the dining hall's ancient, gas-fired oven, using my well-honed concentration to ensure the cookies reached their precise moment of warm, gooey perfection. This instilled an equally warm feeling in the belly of my fellow staff members.

As the first groups of students flowed through our spring programs, I still struggled with the uncertainty of my relationship with Belle and my stagnant spiritual path. Despite earlier feelings of acceptance, I now flip-flopped between feeling great pain at the thought of losing her and feeling numb. My so-called spiritual path felt like treading water as its main focus was to avoid getting sucked into the social stream at LOC. I diligently read the words of Ramana Maharshi, one of the greatest sages of the 20th century, each evening, but even this did nothing to break the mental stalemate. I conserved my energy, but had nothing productive to expend it on.

As nature abhors a vacuum, the distractions of ordinary life began to encroach. I went rock climbing with the staff one weekend, then found myself at the movie theater another. Tired of thoughts which caused me pain, I wanted escape. Rose's warning that "If you need entertainment or escape, you are asleep," gave me pause. I had no plan, no practice, and no inspiration for the spiritual search, but neither did I want to give up.

Life provided an answer. Downhill from the low ropes course was a stream, barely more than twenty feet wide. Standing on a rock by this stream, just watching the sway of the water, I heard rustling in the grass. Turning quickly, I glimpsed a dark, furry mass dart under the rock. Suddenly, baby groundhogs popped out from beneath it. One in the stream to my left, two in the grass to my right, while one eyed me over the rock's edge. I kept as still as the stone I was standing on and watched them waddle around nibbling grass and leaves. Soon, they ventured onto the rock, walked between my feet and even stood on my shoes. Their mom was still under the rock and poked her head out twice to give me a sidelong look. Her fur was sleek and sparkled in the sun around her brown eyes. Why she did not call the pups away from me I did not know, but we shared this space till the pups wandered back into their den. It was a magical few minutes that replaced the dullness in my mind with hope. I knew I had to keep searching. Like Mr. Rose said: "You reach a point where you don't know what else to do, but you have to keep on looking."

Inspired by the wonder of nature, I took to daily walks in the woods. Though working with children was never easy, my job did offer the world's shortest commute. Rather than driving home the moment the school buses departed, I grabbed a notebook and headed for the tree line.

The chaotic screams and laughter of children faded
from memory as the sound of wind and birds filled my
mind. On one of my walks, I recalled our perennial pester-
ing of Mr. Rose to sit in rapport, and how he kept putting
us off. Once, he dropped a puzzling line that lingered
in my memory. He remarked that a person could sit in
rapport with themselves. "This was different from meditation," he said, "as the mind would eventually go blank in
meditation." I noted in my journal that I had no idea what
he was talking about.

Now I began to wonder. Were moments such as
at the beaver pond with Dave instances of rapport? I
believed a spiritual teacher was the catalyst for rapport,
but perhaps that was wrong. Perhaps there was always
something waiting to speak to me if I listened carefully.
Once again, Sadony's *Gates of the Mind* proved particularly
inspiring. Here, he distinguished between a thought and
an intuition:

> All I can state from personal experience is that
> whenever a feeling originates in my nervous
> system without internal cause, whenever I suc-
> ceed at the same time in eliminating all other
> influence, suspending all other sensory reac-
> tions; i.e., when I stop thinking independently
> and allow my thought to be "shaped" by the
> feeling, then what takes place in my imagina-
> tion (though it remains only imagination, com-

posited of my own memories) nevertheless cor-
responds with some external reality or event,
past, present, or future, without any limitation
in space or time save the decided and very
troublesome and insurmountable limitation of
what my memory contains to contribute to the
visualized representation that is the foundation
of my understanding.

I wasn't looking to foretell the future, but I did sense
that sitting in rapport was an intuitive exercise that I could
practice. With notepad and pencil, I sat and waited in the
woods for a feeling to come. I was waiting for a feeling
that seemed to come from outside me. I was not sitting
and concentrating like in meditation (which was no longer
possible for me), but sat with a relaxed attentiveness. I
kept waiting, and the feelings brought forth words—
sometimes only a single word or a line, which threaded
into other words and lines, or might be meaningless. I
imagined myself an animal, soaking in the sun, relaxing
yet attentive to my senses. Bare bones of poem-like
phrases appeared, then later that evening I fleshed out the
images; with luck, holding the feeling that inspired them.
I was trying to feel. Only when I truly reached a point of
knowing nothing else to do, yet still wanting to reach my
goal, did I stumble upon a way forward. It wasn't even a
new way. It was what Belle had encouraged me to do for

years, but only now did I understand. I wrote a poem to celebrate this understanding:

"Spaces"

Lie softly
use your head
to open a gate
in your head.
Between wake and sleep
is a realm
where sights are felt,
and sounds are smelled.
Relax, unwind, but stay awake
take some time to uncreate
this logic, order, sense, and place.
Stop the march, dance instead,
rejoice in the things off the top of your head.

I felt for the first time that I glimpsed the "Invisible Current," the ray of creation from Rose's diagram of Jacob's Ladder. "By his logic man can do nothing," Rose said, "By himself he can do nothing. Unless. Unless man can, through some faculty of feeling, pick up a downward emanation from man's Real Self, or from God, or the Absolute, or from that which you wish to call It..." As the weeks passed, I continued to sit and feel and write in the woods, waiting in the space from which creativity arose.

In mid-October, I drove to the Farm and took a long walk down the nearly dried-up bed of Wheeling Creek. The colors of fall marched up the side of the valley in full display. Little pools lay about the creek bed, decorated with fallen red and yellow leaves. The sun warmed the exposed stone of the creek, and now and then the clack of a creek stone unbalanced by my steps echoed along the hillsides. It was utterly beautiful and serene. Mirage-like, another walker appeared around a bend of the creek. He was taking photographs. I had no idea what to say in such a meeting. I wanted to say nothing, yet share my feelings. We got within a few feet of one another, and he paused.

"Is it always like this, and takes the change of seasons to get us to notice?" he said.

His words were like a depth charge, "Is it always like this?" We stood in silence, I, utterly unable to do justice to his profound comment, or the beauty we drank together.

I entered new ground, unexplored territory, and felt far from life on the Farm despite my frequent visits. Though I went to TAT meetings and volunteered on projects, I felt no one in the group could help me. I was on my own path.

Chapter 11:
Death, Sex, and Darshan

You don't have to go looking for trauma,
it will come to you.

—*Richard Rose*

A few weeks after my magical walk down Wheeling Creek, the phone rang in the LOC office, and a doctor slowly, carefully, explained the results of my brain scan.

Belle had convinced me to visit a physician after almost seven years of near-constant fatigue. I rationalized that too much meditation, corn flakes, and potatoes while on the Farm was partly to blame, but the outdoor exercise and unlimited food at LOC had not countered this neglect. Plus, the fatigue began before I moved to the Farm. It was just so ingrained that I no longer thought of it as a problem. It's who I was—tired when I went to bed and tired when I woke up.

My first round of blood work proved normal, but after a thoughtful, beard-scratching pause the doctor suggested more tests. His hunch revealed elevated levels of a hormone, and an MRI of the brain precipitated the phone call: it was a pituitary tumor.

I knew nothing of the pituitary, but this pea-sized gland in the center of my skull pumped out nine different hormones. One of them was more than three hundred times the norm. The offending molecule was prolactin—best known for enabling milk production, and sometimes described as the "nesting hormone." As prolactin increased testosterone decreased, so while many of Rose's students struggled to remain celibate and sit quietly, I was apparently a monk by virtue of my hormones as much as will-power.

Given Rose's emphasis on celibacy, a mega dose of prolactin might seem a shortcut to enlightenment, but this missed part of his formula. The purpose of celibacy was to build up the energy normally spent in sexual activity and redirect it. Like transforming the energy of anger by going for a run or hitting a punching bag, Rose advocated trans-muting one's natural sexual energy. Rather than running up a hill, one applied the sexual energy to mental efforts in a spiritual direction—like reading a book or meditating. In my case, however, there was nothing to transmute.

Though the tumor was likely benign, it would keep growing if untreated, crushing the optic nerve, destroying all my hormone function, leading to blindness, then death. The first line of treatment was medication, and as I lingered for weeks in the purgatory of prescriptions, consultations and more blood tests, a new determination filled me. The question "what am I?" became more practical and important than ever before. I tested the edges of my mind for the feeling of anything in the universe other than me—a God, spirit, or something. The pain of death did not scare me, as logic said the pain would end with the body. It was the tremendous unknown of *after* death that frightened me, and that fear became motivation.

For two months death was again my chief motivator. In that stark light, my attachments to life became obvious: 1) The love of another human. 2) The love of nature. 3) The love of self.

First there was the love of another person, which I had sought for years. My failed relationships showed I was powerless in this regard. Even if I did meet someone and we swore to love forever, the example of my father's unexpected death taught the impermanence of such love. My father was here one day and gone the next, never to be seen again.

The love of nature was my most visible attachment, but I felt that falling away. I wasn't trying to drop it, but even sitting quietly in the woods with life/energy/whatever-it-was flowing through me like electricity, the transience and limitation of all things was undeniable. The "I" that received these mighty feelings was like a leaf shaking in the wind, and I was completely identified as that leaf which would soon fall from the tree and rot.

The last attachment was the love of self. It was impossible to imagine life without that attachment, though poems came to me that hinted at the feeling:

Do I carry my soul
Or does my soul carry me?
In the crowded stations of my life
How often do I hear the symphony of Me.
How often do I care to listen,
How often is the past the present,
How often must I be reminded
By the wind in the trees?

I learned something else about facing death. After I told LOC's director about the tumor, he introduced me to a friend with cancer. David was outgoing and energetic, a fine art photographer with nothing to his name other than chutzpah and talent. He invited me over for dinner with his girlfriend and her two young children. It was a perfectly normal evening, except for the question I asked as we said our goodbyes in the street. "How do you live with the intensity of knowing death is ever present?"

"You forget," he said, "You go back to watching television. The mind can't keep that thought indefinitely. You get used to it and go back to your routine."

It was bewildering, but true. I labored under a daily forgetting of my deepest desire. In the face of a condition which could kill me, I found myself wasting time rather than spending every waking moment seeking my true identity. My mind would not hold that intensity day in and day out.

I carried that thought with me as I drove to Raleigh for a December reunion of SKS friends: Eric, Danny, Georg, Doug, Bill, Alex, and others. Five years earlier, we each wrote a "letter to our self," and now we met once again in Harrelson Hall to open these time capsules. All we needed was a campfire to complete the feeling of a rendezvous of explorers. Each of us took turns speaking, trying to condense five years into as many minutes. Most were still involved in the SKS and the search for enlightenment to some degree. I, however, had left the confines of the SKS, and even Rose, to venture into the unknown. I had no group or system to claim allegiance to. After the final speaker, papers rustled as we opened our letters and silently read them. Mine was plain and short:

Where I want to be

To have the ability to touch and not be touched, to have superior concentration, to be a vector toward truth, to know enough to help others spiritually, to be a stand-alone seeker, and to no longer fear death.

I read my list to the rest of the group. I felt I had achieved nothing on it, though each goal was still in focus and attainable. I wanted all my energy directed to the spiritual search, and to be helpful to others yet dependent on no one. "To touch and not be touched" was a nod to Rose's concept of between-ness, which was to act without attachment to the outcome. And that bit about not fearing death? That was both perceptive and naïve—going to the heart of the problem, but having no idea how deeply ingrained it was.

Others read aloud their letters, and our sharing wove stories of youthful longing and dawning resignation. We were still twenty-somethings but edging towards thirty, and relationships, jobs, and the other so-called practical matters of life were on the horizon. I had created a life as free from these distractions as possible, but sensed that wouldn't last forever. The window of opportunity was narrowing. Georg called the meeting to a close, and I lingered outside Harrelson Hall as we said our goodbyes. I watched as each friend walked away, their story fading into the night. These were my first real friends—relationships grounded in honesty—the people with whom I awoke to the spiritual search. All of us were infected by a peculiar longing for truth that bonded us like old soldiers.

Back at LOC, Belle reached out to me in a final attempt to build a romantic relationship. She felt such a relationship was the next step on her spiritual path, but my feeling for her now was more akin to a sister than a lover. I wanted friendship, and the thought of marriage and children was of no interest. At the same time, a part of me selfishly did not want to see her with another man. I toyed with the idea of "married life." As if trying it on for size, I house-sat for a married friend one week and enjoyed the fruits of his middle-class life: a house with a yard in a quiet neighborhood, an easy chair and television, and cupboards filled with snacks. If I were sitting in *my* easy chair, in *my* house, with *my* children running around upstairs, would this fill the emptiness in my heart? It did not feel that way. The mysterious "I" at the center of "my" life was the constant problem. Still, I delayed—not wanting to lose Bell's friendship, yet not wanting to advance our relationship. It was a slow rip rather than a clean cut.

Perversely, as I grew stronger about what I did not want and turned ever more to the spiritual path as the only answer, my practice became desert dry. Perhaps it was winter, yet again, exercising its cold hand over my mood. I continued to write poetry, connecting with feelings of despair and hope, and vague intimations of eternality, yet these poems were the extent of my spiritual work:

"Kneeling to God"

Stop reading these poems.
You know what to do.
Divest your self of the you.

Retire from the stage.
Lock yourself away five minutes a day,
and weep for your nothingness.
Be ground to dust
by the weight of eternity.
Be dust.

There had to be something more I could do, but
winter dragged on without inspiration. No books could
break my mood and there was no one to talk to about such
things other than the occasional visit with Belle. I installed
special grow lights in my room, hoping the increased light
spectrum would help my mood, but nothing changed.
Even the threat of my tumor failed to focus my mind. At
last warmer days arrived, and I sat outside and relaxed.
Poems once more flowed easily, but I felt no closer to
discovering their origin.

LOC shut down for spring break, so I spent the week
in Kentucky and visited my 92-year-old grandfather for
an unexpected dose of Zen. Year after year, our unvarying
interaction began with him reclining his easy chair, and
then lecturing me on the importance of getting a good job
with a pension. "You should teach school," was his typical
refrain. After that, he recited stories of people from his life
till I lost track of who did what and where.

This visit, though, his recitation was striking rather
than dull. Line by line, stories of life and death wrapped
me into their short-lived drama.

"Two miles down from my farm, that place was owned by Sumner," my grandfather said, rocking his chair to the story's cadence.

"Now, he had a son, Paul, who married a girl from Buckner. I taught her Spanish in high school. They had two sons." His chair slowed ever so slightly.

"Paul was in tractor equipment sales. Worked at a big dealership in Mount Sterling. He died." There was a long pause. "There's houses on that farm now. I don't know what happened to the kids." He paused again and looked at me unblinking. The room was alive with feeling, even the dust motes sparkling in the afternoon sun. His palms lay folded on his chest, as if an invisible hand of cards was yet to be revealed. Was this pause the void rising up to swallow us both, or simply the aged firing of his neurons?

He began again, recounting the Mason family, then the Adairs; he went on: children, neighbors, students, friends, fathers, brothers. He held me spell-bound for forty-five minutes recounting these intersections of his life with others—lived here, worked there, married so and so, had children, then died. Always, inevitably, they died. Grandfather stopped the tale and looked at me again in silence, lips pursed. "Well, let's get something to eat," he said. With that, he levered himself out of the easy chair and took my awaiting arm.

All stories ended in the graveyard. How could it be that I would end the same? Wasn't I special? Death was so inconceivable that my mind's reaction was to think it would live forever. My mind knew that I could not, but refused to consider the thought for more than a moment.

July arrived and marked my 30th birthday, which I celebrated with an afternoon nap. A quiet clarity arose as my mind drifted toward sleep, and it became painfully obvious that all I cherished and delineated as me would die. My personality was doomed. My demarcation was just a line in the sand near a rising ocean. What was I without my personality? Wide awake, yet unmoving as if suspended in space, all I knew was I must find an answer. To live in this unknowing, death facing me, was unbearable. Three hours later the mood was a memory as I engaged with life again—driving in traffic and making plans for the future. Nothing had really changed since my conversation with David. Despite my determination, I was engaged in an endless cycle of momentarily waking up, then falling back into forgetful sleep. Rose, in fact, labeled "forgetting" the fourth faculty of the mind, with perception, retention, and reaction being the other three.

At least I was aware of this predicament. I was no longer building a better ego and had moved beyond additive practices. Instead, if I even had a practice it was one of ever increasing ignorance. Not a day passed without the startling thought "Who am I?" "What is going on?" "What is to become of me?" or "What is this place?" I had no answers and felt utterly incomplete. I wanted to know something for sure, to have a feeling of certainty to share with others, but I had nothing.

Rose once said that a depressed person had a more realistic view of the world. I had that going for me, so perhaps there was cause for hope.

Looking to shake up my mental stalemate, I went to the movie theater. It wasn't a novel idea. Rose noticed as a young man how he would step into a movie theater in one mood, then later emerge feeling he could conquer the world. The movie I chose moved my mood in an unforeseen way. *Saving Private Ryan* absorbed me in its opening minutes as a company of soldiers stormed Omaha beach on D-Day. The first person point of view of the camera swayed, assaulting my senses with explosions, screams and bullet fire, and then silence as the camera dipped under the water only to plow onward into the chaos. My emotions lurched forward with the view, utterly entrancing me. I winced at the randomness of death, the maelstrom of battle, and any hope that life was in my control bled away in the sand. As the movie progressed, death peeled away character after character—there were no rules distinguishing the worthy from the unworthy, there was no magic hand protecting us. We could all die at any moment. The lights rose in the theater, but I was spellbound and too stunned to move for several minutes. My chest felt empty and hollow. All I cherished was nothing, yet in that feeling of emptiness was something beautiful and freeing. I felt wraith-like, as if light and wind blew through my insubstantial form.

I drove to Belle's apartment in this otherworldly mood, but the feeling vanished within minutes of lying on the couch — as this clear sky filled with the advancing storm front of the ego, and thoughts and feelings of self roiled about in a self-made wind. Why did the beauty of nothingness come and go? Why did my ego rise again?

Looking to repeat this experience the following week, I returned to the same theater and watched the film again. There was no deep impact the second time. I learned an element of surprise was necessary for a shock to deeply strike.

I was soon surprised by another event, as my medication at long last began to shrink the tumor. My prolactin level dropped and testosterone rose. As these hormones changed, I witnessed anew the depths to which I had no control over thoughts.

I first detected this shift during a long autumn walk to the lake, where Dave and I had stood during his wild run in the woods the prior year. At the edge of the lake was a massive, fallen white oak which the park staff sawed through to keep the trail open. I stopped to count the tree rings, and by the time I reached two hundred and thirty-five my mind had fallen into a reflective mood. I realized my energy was slowly increasing along with my sexual interest. For the first time in years, I found myself noticing when a woman was near. I hadn't suddenly

decided I wanted to pay attention to women. It was
if a forgotten antenna was reactivating. Women were
"interesting" and when I was around them the thought of
whether they were reciprocating my interest predominated. This, as I recalled from my teenage years, was what
it meant to be a "normal" heterosexual guy. To see my
desires in motion was extraordinary. While I was used to
the dance of thoughts emerging one after another from
the mind's darkened corners, it was something new to see
my desires change. Even more amazing was my powerless
witnessing of this shift.

This was more than just a movie-inspired mood.
Depressed moods, peaceful moods, and happy moods
were colored gels that lay over experience. Moods passed
within minutes, hours, or at most days. One of my fail-safe
rules was to "never make a decision in a mood," because
the mood would soon change. There were deeper states of
conviction, however. Rose differentiated between moods
and the stronger beliefs he called states of mind. A state
of mind was a core conviction only questioned under
extraordinary circumstances. It was a way of seeing the
world and my self in that world. If moods were like the
lighting on a movie set, then a state of mind was like the
script. Sexual desire was a state of mind missing from my
script, but had now rumbled to life. Rather than seeing
women as people, a filter descended that first asked some
variation of, "Are they sexually available?" This objectifi-
cation was as lamentable as it was relentlessly powerful.

My increased sexual energy ushered in complementary interests. I began lifting weights for the first time in seven years. I began thinking of leaving LOC, and a desire arose to prove myself in the world by making a lot of money. If such a thought had appeared a year earlier I would have dismissed it like my retreat-escaping daydreams of becoming a baker. Even more amazing was that such a thought would never have appeared!

Amidst this bubbling stew, Danny and I learned of Mother Meera. Stories of this Indian guru told of her transmitting or inducing a spiritual experience through "darshan." I loosely understood this term as a ceremonial meeting with the guru in which they bestowed a blessing or energy that changed the consciousness of the recipient. Despite the pitfalls of chasing transmission, I did it anyway. Within weeks, Danny and I were on a flight to Germany to visit the guru.

In a little village amidst a countryside dotted with castles, well over one hundred and fifty people gathered outside of Mother Meera's expansive home to partake of her darshan. Everyone was very quiet and serious as Danny and I stood and waited, shuffling forward in a long line till we entered the house. Once inside we were not allowed to stand, so a line of crouching, kneeling, and sitting aspirants snaked down hallways and around corners, and another hour passed as we shambled towards the guru. Finally I was in a meeting hall in the bowels of the house, where thirty or forty people sat in chairs facing Meera at the center of the room. She was an utterly ordinary-looking Indian woman in her thirties, except for the line of people kneeling in front of her. I worked my way up the aisle, then knelt before Meera. As I touched her feet, she held her hands over my head, then I looked up and gazed into her eyes. My vision was a little hazy, as if there was a fog between us. I strained my senses for any hint of profundity or electricity in the air, but the feeling was completely unremarkable. My ten seconds were over, and I was ushered away.

One darshan down and six more to go. There were no other meetings and no discussions, just waiting till the next day's darshan. Leaving the hall, we met a couple of young English ladies who were quite happy to meet a couple of American guys. The next evening, Danny was making out with one of them outside our room while I, despite my testosterone surge, was scared to death the other would appear for me. I escaped that evening, but we joined them for lunch a couple of times. I'd never met this sort of spiritual seeker. They seemed like tourists collecting stories of spiritual adventures. If they heard about sadhus on the Ganges or a new type of meditation, they would hop on a plane and go for a visit. I felt lucky to have Rose's single-minded intensity as my model for the spiritual search, though I saw the irony in my hopping on a plane to chase Mother Meera.

We attended six more darshans, but Meera's gaze was ever non-impressive to both Danny and me. Since I couldn't feel her presence, I decided to test if she could feel mine. On the final night, I filled my head with thoughts of disgust with the darshan scene and gave her a challenging stare. Her placid face did not change. She was either completely in bliss or completely oblivious, and I cynically concluded the latter. Thus ended my week with Mother Meera. Surveying the long line of seekers—sitting with hands in prayer, in full lotus, half lotus, kneeling, focused on their breath, saying japas, finding chakras, feeling vibrations, quieting their minds, trying to look humble and pious—Danny called us "a bunch of desperate people." That certainly applied to me. Nearly a year after my tumor diagnosis, I'd gone from facing death to facing a new state of mind. I had little idea what was next.

Chapter 12:
The Hunt

Work like hell when the door opens.

— Richard Rose

Returning from Germany without enlightenment or even a wisp of inspiration, my first acts were to purchase a computer and internet access. It was stocks and mutual funds, rather than spiritual teachers, which had my attention. I was dreaming of a new life, and whatever presented itself to me was of interest. So much so that evenings found me doing pull-ups and calf raises to train for a rock climb with our new assistant director Jeff. His contagious enthusiasm lured me into my first multi-pitch climb—the four hundred foot Great Arch at Stone Mountain, North Carolina. Though I intended it as nothing other than a fun experience, it became another instance of life as a teacher.

The stark granite dome of Stone Mountain rose from the surrounding forest like a gray wave. Marring its smooth surface was a scimitar-like scar curving from left to right as if a giant flake of stone was torn from its face. This was the Great Arch. Jeff and I climbed it as a team, he taking the lead as I belayed him to a first set of metal rings bolted to the mountain's face. There, he clipped his climbing harness to the rings, then belayed me as I stepped up to follow his route. I placed my fingers in the crack to my left, then simultaneously stood on my right foot and leaned back. Weight pulled against my arms into the empty space behind me and simultaneously pushed the sticky sole of my climbing shoe into the stone. Between the empty space and stone, I began to move—raising up on one leg, then reaching for the next hand hold.

As I gained height, the mind filled with sensations of motion and pressure, dancing and tension, freedom and fear. Wind gently whistled through the slots in my helmet. Heat rose from patches of speckled granite warmed by the sun. Carabiners jingled with each step. Thoughts fell away as the world shrank to cracks and crevices, the angle of a handhold, and the surety of the next foot placement. Thus absorbed, I climbed till Jeff and I were side by side. "Dude," he quietly said, "Awesome." Not that I was awesome, but everything—this place and this moment—was awesome. He was strong and competent on the rock, completely in tune with the art of the climb. We passed two more pitches, then walked up the final slope to the summit. There in the shade of a small tree, we watched vultures rise on thermals—feeling wind in feathers and the urge to rise higher and higher. There was no need to talk. Vibrant, beautiful alive. Zen.

I could have lingered an hour, but Jeff's restless energy pulled us onward. Just as we climbed in segments, we rappelled down likewise. Jeff went first, gradually disappearing over the descending curve of the mountain. Suddenly I felt very alone, four hundred feet in the air and facing two stainless steel rings bolted into the granite. My task was simple: connect myself to the climbing rope with my rappelling device (called an ATC), then disconnect the leash attaching me to the rings, and be on my way. Hanging from those two little rings, with no sound except the wind, a fear-filled thought hit me: what if I dropped my ATC? If that happened, it seemed I might as well be on the moon. Jeff could not climb up to me and no one else was around. The smooth flow of my task broke into disjointed movements. A suddenly sweaty hand gripped the ATC. "Move the rope," I said, focusing on each step, as if reciting a script: move rope, clip carabiners, unclip the leash. Focusing pushed the fear away, and I rappelled down to Jeff without further drama. Two more rappels brought us to the bottom.

After lunch, I wished I was back on the Great Arch. With its many cracks and ledges, it seemed far safer than the featureless expanses of stone we tackled next. This was friction climbing—a nerve-chewing subset of climbing that relied on the sticking power of climbing shoes and the traction from the palms of our hands keeping us from

179

sliding. Bolts provided places to clip in a rope and arrest a fall, but the "long runouts" between each bolt meant a wickedly big fall from one bolt to the next.

Unfortunately, the *first* bolt to clip in was twenty-five feet up the smooth slab. I stood helplessly while Jeff glued himself to the granite slope. He was at the edge of his skill, delicately balancing while carefully raising one arm above his head to clip to the bolt. Doubt flooded my mind. Why take this risk to climb a rock? What are we doing here? Once clipped in, he gracefully executed the rest of the climb, and I lowered him to the ground. It was then my turn to climb up and recover the leashes he clipped to the bolts and rappel down.

My heart was drained of enthusiasm, yet I was ostensibly living a life of accepting challenges and striving to do my best. Jeff and I had talked on the drive down about the importance of giving one hundred percent to one's endeavors. Caught between rhetoric and reality, I chose to climb.

From the first step, I knew I wasn't ready for this beast. Like standing on ice, I was just waiting for the fall. Every foothold seemed unsecure, while the pain of a granite rock face shredding my skin and nose became ever more certain. This panic-provoking thought grew stronger as I climbed higher. "Jesus, fuck, shit," I whispered over and over. My body wanted to stop, yet I climbed until I faced two stainless steel rings embedded in the granite.

Pausing to review my next moves, I sensed a darkness at the edge of my awareness. It wasn't outside me, yet it wasn't me either. It felt like a black mass or cloud inside my mind. I immediately knew it was fear, and that if I entertained it or focused on it I was doomed. This blackness teased my attention with the thought "what if?" What if I drop my ATC? What if my leash does not hold? What if I drop the rope? If I turned and embraced any of these thoughts, if I looked into that blackness, I would panic and fail. Pushing away these deadly thoughts, I started quietly whistling and turned my focus away from the looming presence at the edge of my awareness. Whistle and move, whistle and move. I made the transfer from rope to leash and from leash to rappel. In a minute I was back on the ground—but the strain of my desperate focus left me utterly unmanned. Jeff asked if I was alright, but I just limply shook my head and stared at the ground. That was our last climb of the day.

For days I studied what to make of this. I felt like a child who saw a bedroom monster and hid under the covers. In my journal I wrote:

> I feel defeated, unmanned, unsure of my willpower. I came too close to breaking under the stress, saw too much of my fragility, my weakness. Again, my sense of self, of wholeness, of competence, is weakened. I feel closer to insanity than greatness.

Eventually I saw this unmanned feeling as humbling rather than humiliating. I had experienced the limitations of the body and mind—my self—and the end of a fantasy of invincibility. I began to understand that humiliation was a product of a false face being exposed, but not admitting the truth of the exposure. Denial of the truth led to humiliation. Humility was the product of an admission of truth. I was humbled, not by a decision to seek humility, but by coming to the edge of my capacity and witnessing the cracks in self-perception. I witnessed a body in turmoil, saw my will striving to save itself, and observed the mind invaded by an entity called fear. What was left that I could claim as me? Rather than controlling more and more of my life, perhaps my only power was a limited ability to turn away from certain thoughts. A painful truth was setting me free.

I felt a dying and shedding oncoming, which meant a new birth as well. The arc of my life across Kentucky, North Carolina, West Virginia, and Pennsylvania was ending, and the future lay elsewhere. It was time to employ serious medicine: the geographic cure.

I hatched a plan to tour the country searching for a place to start a group. Rose thought different cities had a feel or energy to them—there was spiritual possibility in some places and a darkness over others. Through reading and guesswork my list of candidates narrowed to Charlottesville, VA; Austin, TX; San Francisco, CA; and Boulder,

CO. I hoped for an intuitive feel that one would be my new home. In the meantime, I had goodbyes to say.

I paid a final visit to Mr. Rose. The man who once led me up and down hills on the Farm now tottered the halls of a nursing home. We sat together for a few minutes, though I knew nothing to do other than smile and nod as he told me tales of nonsense. A nurse brought over a tray of food and Rose leapt up. "Watch your feet!" he warned and grabbed the tray as if wrestling a heavy plate of metal. I could not imagine the phantasms that his disintegrating mind perceived. Rising to leave, I offered my hand which he took in an iron grip. "Thank you," he said, looking me dead in the eye. Even then, his effect on me was unsettling and doubt-raising—which one of us was more deluded?

A few days later, I wrote Belle a long-delayed letter telling her I no longer felt our relationship would work. The letter was a formality, really only for myself, as she had met someone else and told me she felt perfect with him. I think she stuck around despite my waffling, just long enough to help me through the tumor. Thus our years together ended with a whimper. By turns angry and at peace, I sadly mused over a long list of experiences we would never share. It seemed I was still holding on to porch swing and lemonade dreams.

A tiny going away party in Moundsville marked me as one of a long line of those come and gone at the Farm. Mr. Rose's wife Cecy tried to be upbeat, but I felt somber.

I had rolled the dice for enlightenment, but failed. I did not blame Rose, though. The failure was all mine.

Just days before my departure, I traveled to Princeton, N.J., to meet my old Zen Den pal Eric and attend a workshop by Douglas Harding. I had read Harding's *On Having No Head*, but his idea of our inherent "Headlessness" made no sense as the head sitting atop my body was quite obvious. Despite this, Harding's unique voice and concepts, and the prospect of visiting Eric, roused my curiosity enough to make the five-hour journey to Princeton.

Eric and I joined twenty or thirty people in a small classroom for the "Headless Workshop." I strained to tune my mental radio to any "feelings" in the air. Harding rose from a seat in the front row, and immediately enchanted me with his British accent. He was at once self-assured and self-deprecating, scholarly and a common man. I saw hints of Mr. Rose in his stocky frame, balding white hair, and boundless energy for discussion. At ninety years of age, Douglas (as everyone called him) had a remarkable grasp of quotations and a sense of humor which brought the most flighty esoteric ideas down to the practical matter of everyday living.

The workshop was a mix of talk and his unique experiments. With Douglas guiding, I sat across from Eric for the Tube experiment. With a tube concocted from a paper grocery bag with one end cut out, we leaned our heads forward so our faces covered each end of the tube.

Looking at the far end, I saw Eric's face. Douglas's gravelly voice explained what was next.

"Ignore your thoughts, memories, and feelings," Douglas said. "Be freshly aware of what you see. Study this other face."

My eyes at first nervously glanced at Eric's face. The affect was intimate, but I ignored my initial thoughts and dove in, looking closely at his features without mental comment.

Douglas continued. "Is there any reason to be afraid? Where is your consciousness? Where is your partner's consciousness? Is there any reason why your consciousness cannot contain his, why your consciousness is not his?"

Douglas' questions led my awareness to the far side of the tube. My awareness was expanding, yet becoming less clearly defined as "me."

"He is you. He is you." The words "He is you" sent chills up my spine. Douglas' words trailed off as if he, too, was caught in the profundity of the moment. I briefly felt that Eric was me. Not that I knew his thoughts, but that this awareness was in both of us.

"All of life is confrontation, but where is the need to confront now?"

"Nowhere," I realized, "I love this person."

We lowered the tube and an unspoken glow remained, though my logical mind yammered underneath the experience, seeking to question Douglas' approach.

"I don't 'get' Headlessness. What are you saying?" I later asked.

"Well," Douglas said, "what did you see at your end of the tube?"

"Nothing."

"There. Don't try to deny what you saw. It is the truth."

My mind rebelled at the thought…

The next day Eric and I visited Douglas and his wife Catherine at the home of the workshop organizer. Amazingly, no one else from the workshop was there. Only a couple from New York who missed the workshop took advantage of this opportunity. The seven of us sat in the backyard under a shade tree for a magical two and a half hours.

Douglas, in the same T-shirt and dress pants as the day before, was at ninety far more animated in his speech than I at thirty. Like Rose, there was a deep presence about him. When he stared at me, as I learned he often did after making a point, his eyes seemed infinitely deep, and I felt he knew my every thought. Whether enlightened or not, this realization of Headlessness had given him everything he wanted.

"Everything my heart could desire is to be found in the center," he said.

I questioned him about enlightenment, and his answer was refreshingly confrontational.

"So Shawn here is after enlightenment, which is way up here, while what Douglas is talking about is way down here. So Shawn will forget about what is right here and go after enlightenment. I wish you luck."

"Enlightenment is a loaded word which I think is best avoided," he said.

Douglas found that people confused enlightenment with perfection of the personality and commented that, "Perfection of the human is not attainable."

I asked if it is possible to reach an end to wondering who you are.

"Knowing who you are is attainable."

"Are results proportionate to energy applied?" I asked, referring to a principle from Rose's teachings.

"I wouldn't say results are proportionate to the amount of practice, but rather to the passion. You have to have a passion for this. You can have anything you desire if you have passion."

Though impressed, I was suspicious of Douglas' point that confrontation dissolves in Headlessness. Was this a saintly façade, or some kind of loving-kindness fantasy?

"What would you do if you faced a physical confrontation?" I asked.

"Let's say someone comes at me with a sword and says, 'Douglas, I'm going to cut off your no-head.' What will I do? I don't know. Perhaps I will say, 'Go ahead, I've lived long enough.' Perhaps I will punch them in the nose.

I can't say. This is not staged. There's not a preconceived set of rules. There are no rules. I don't know what will happen until I see what Douglas does. Why don't you go ahead and try me and we'll see what happens?"

I declined the invitation, satisfied that Douglas was not posing behind a wobbly framework of words.

Our exchange was remarkably reminiscent of being with Mr. Rose: inspiring, frustrating, challenging, humorous, and real. As we prepared to leave I noticed Douglas looking at us, shaking his head. I wondered what he saw.

Days later, I made my way westward from LOC, stopping in Kentucky where Uncle Terry left me with an apropos quote: "A wise man is nothing but a fool with a good memory."

From Kentucky, I drove to Austin, TX, which immediately impressed me as a vibrant, youthful town. The campus felt like a place where students would appreciate an SKS-style group. Content with my first impressions, I drove to San Antonio to meet a spiritual teacher named Metta Zetty.

Though I thought myself spiritually well-read, I was unfamiliar with teachers from the "you are already enlightened" school. Metta was firmly in this class, and I was as puzzled as if she told me to jump to the moon when she suggested to "Imagine that you have arrived and everything is perfect as it is." This sounded like the sort of practice Rose warned against when he said to avoid imagination in meditation.

"Pay attention to the 'now,'" Metta said. I listened and nodded my head, but refused to believe her. If this was true, what about all my years of searching? Enlightenment was supposed to be a monumental effort and the result of extreme tension. I was certain it could not be found by simply imagining I was already enlightened. Of course that certainty was a little set of beliefs for which I had no proof.

Though I sensed her conviction and she seemed serene, even happy, I did not feel the same depth as Rose, Bernadette Roberts, or Douglas Harding. Metta did make me wonder if the path had to be as hard as it seemed. Looking back, I see Metta Zetty was a foretaste of the explosion of "teachers of the now" that pervade today's landscape. For most, the "now" they teach of has been subtly inhabited by the same old self. But that's a story for another day.

From San Antonio, I headed west across Texas aiming to meet Alex in New Mexico. As naïve as a greenhorn pioneer, I belatedly realized that all the pleasant-looking green patches marked in my road atlas were actually treeless, sunbaked slabs of hardpan. It was too hot to stop and set-up camp, so I drove till evening, finally pulling into a state park that was little more than boulders and dirt. As night deepened, I watched two guys with canvas bags and headlamps hunt for rattlesnakes amidst the rocks. I zipped my tent tightly for the night.

More hot country awaited the next day, but I was hopeful that New Mexico's Isleta Lakes campground was as enticing as its name. At the campground office, the clerk asked me twice if I wanted a campground pass, then handed it to me with a look of reluctance. Something was amiss, and as I drove through the campground it dawned on me that everyone was either a Native American or Hispanic. Suddenly, every glance in my direction felt like a stare, and I imagined some unspoken rule was broken. I was so used to a "white" world that anything different seemed threatening. I drove slowly out the way I came in, too embarrassed to ask for a refund. My loving experience in Harding's tube was nowhere to be found.

I reached Taos the next day, and found a landscape of dreams and artists. The dun-colored houses and ground blended into one another, as if generation after generation of people, hills, trees, rocks, and land were becoming one. I met Alex at his parents' home, much of which they built themselves out of adobe. Their house was all soft edges, at once rising up and crumbling back into the earth, and so much like the hands that built it.

Alex shared all that was beautiful with his home. We spent the night on a trampoline in the front yard under a clear and cold sky. Huddled in sleeping bags, Alex mused that a pleasant childhood made one forever nostalgic of that place. The wide skies and stone of the Southwest were not home to me, but the deep black night with range upon range of stars pulled forth memories.

As a little child, I tilted back my head and stared at a star-filled night sky. I was alone in our back yard. What first appeared like a flat field of stars, grew deeper and deeper the longer I stared. Drawn into the depths, I felt my legs wobble as if I would fall at any moment. As Alex talked, I felt that falling once again, only now I recognized it was both falling backwards into whatever was behind me and upwards into the stars. It was as if inside and outside were merging into one. But it was only "as if." The merging wasn't complete. Wherever I went, I kept dragging my self with me—that seemingly intractable spectator of all that happened. What was that self? That night, I realized that in spite of thinking my spiritual path a failure I still wanted answers.

With time running short, I decided against visiting San Francisco and drove to Boulder, Colorado. Alas, I found it homogeneously hip and too rich for its own good. I met an old hippie on a bench, an observer of people, with interests in shamanism and alternative healing. He said there was a center for every major religion in town, yet he did not feel a strong spiritual sense… and the rent was really steep. Leaving Boulder, I detoured to the Rocky Mountains to visit Bob F., who returned to those high lands after his Farm days. From sweltering in San Antonio a few days ago, I then stood far above the tree line on a thin crust of snow. Everywhere I looked were mountains stacked one after another, and a deep wanderlust begged me to seek the unseen behind the top of every rock and around the corner of every bend. I understood why Bob returned to this place.

From the Rockies, I threaded back through the flat lands of Kansas on my way to Kentucky. There was a magical night camped at a state park by a Kansas lake. At sunset, mayflies floated over the lake's mirrored surface, which was broken now and then by the splash of a fish leaping for a meal. Each splash was like the clack of a wooden block in a silent world. Striking, purifying, clarifying. Zen. Was Metta right? Was the answer right here—now? Or was Douglas right, that there was nothing where I thought there was something? Or were the stars telling me the truth? Or was I just a frightened white boy, a robot programmed to run from all that was different from him? Despite the questions, I was not without hope for answers as I continued through Missouri, Illinois, and Indiana, finally arriving in Kentucky.

Reviewing the trip, Austin appealed to me as the place to settle and form a group. I could hunt my fortune too, as the dot-com internet boom was in full force. Before moving to Austin, however, I had a meeting with Douglas Harding in England. I wasn't done with his simple yet perplexing experiments in Headlessness.

Chapter 13:
A Week of Headlessness

*How is it that we need all this prodding, all these warnings
and earnest invitation and promises of infinite rewards,
to persuade us to take a really close look at ourselves?*

—Douglas Harding

For me, there was nothing quite like a plane ride for bringing death to the forefront. As the plane lifted off bound for England, I had visions of sleepy airplane mechanics dropping nuts and bolts into engines. At least with a car my hands were on the steering wheel, giving a sense of being in control despite the hundreds of other out-of-control drivers around me. On a plane, I was totally out of control of the multitude of mistakes that could plummet us into the earth. And yet, although I was very aware of this total lack of control, I refused to relax into the truth of the situation. Just like Ramana Marharshi's story of train passengers who carried luggage on their heads rather than sit it on the floor and let the train carry it, I couldn't let go of my burden. Bound by attachment to self, the fear of death exposed the excruciating depth of my ignorance. What did it mean to be dead? Would my awareness survive? Maybe I was dead already? If *I* died how would this *I* ever know of its death? Was death infinity—an infinite, eternal moment? Like a house collapsing in flames, these questions tumbled out of the mind, splintered logic, and lodged as burning embers in my chest. Only as the plane leveled out from its ascent did the frantic questions cool. Within minutes of this terror I closed my eyes. "I want to be truly alive to what is real," was the last thought before the drone of the engines lulled me into slumber.

I met Douglas for a two-day workshop, but this was just a prelude to the one-on-one meeting I desired. After a few friendly inquiries I found myself shepherded to his home in Nacton. An architect by trade, the open floor plan and ample windows of Douglas' home were as welcoming as he and his wife Catherine. Situated on a green lot surrounded by high hedges, there was the sense of being on an island. There I was gratefully stranded for several days along with a cigarette-smoking and sake-drinking Zen abbot.

I immersed myself in Douglas' way of life—a way of "seeing" that was grounded in what he called the first-person perspective. We normally imagined ourselves in the third person perspective which was how others saw us: a body with a head on it, separate from all that surrounded it. Douglas challenged me to look at the space I looked out of, the first-person perspective, and answer "What do you see?" He spoke of the immediate experience rather than the imaginative reaction to that experience: the first person versus the third person perspective. His numerous experiments pointed the attention at this space.

The simplest of these experiments was to point a finger at the space I looked out from, where I assumed I had a head, and notice what was there. Looking where my finger pointed, what did I see? The eye attempted to looks backwards, but failed to do so. However, the attempt shifted attention, as if the momentum of the effort shocked the awareness from its lamination to the senses. I couldn't just think through the exercise like a mind game; I had to point and look. The awareness separated from the eye's sensory perception, broke its spell-bound obsession with the external world, and became aware of the space from which I looked. Normally, I was oblivious to that space. Before meeting Douglas, I perceived either an outer world of things or my inner world of thought and awareness—a solid boundary between me and the other. Douglas's experiment shook this boundary.

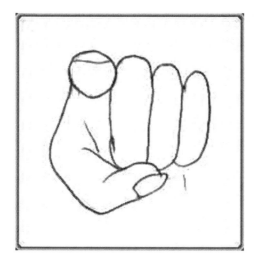

When I honestly looked, there was no head in the space from which I perceived the world. There was an empty stage, a space occupied by the objects of the world. This was the Headless Way—at once obvious but overlooked (like suddenly noticing the feel of pavement under my feet), but also curiously objectionable in light of my beliefs. While I glimpsed the nothingness that Douglas said was our true nature (our first-personhood he called it), I doubted this was enlightenment. Where was the earth-shattering conviction that left no need to continue practicing a technique? My reaction to seeing was "Yeah, but..."

Douglas countered that seeing *is* enlightenment, though he preferred not to use that word. My doubt was typical resistance to the seeing, he said. The third person (the little Shawn) continually raised such questions and concerns.

Glimpsing my nothingness, then second-guessing it and peppering Douglas with questions was my pattern for the week. Douglas' answers repeatedly guided me to seeing without doubt, but as soon as I was alone questions arose again.

I did not question Douglas' authenticity, though, as I glimpsed his everyday life. He had a self-effacing humor, for example, swearing to a natural laziness despite being quite active. Douglas kept busy reading and making sketches in preparation for a workshop in France, and in cooking three meals a day for the assorted people who appeared and disappeared throughout the week. Typically, he wore a t-shirt spotted with stains from preparing meals and marks from the blue pens with which he sketched. Old people become a caricature of their life's focus, and Douglas was clearly about Headlessness—living it, seeing it, and sharing it. In between working, reading, and an occasional snooze, he did his best to help me.

"Remember you have a long habit of not-seeing," he said. The key was to stick with the seeing until "seeing becomes natural."

As for why he stuck with it: "I think what's kept my eye on the ball these sixty years is having something to do. Devising experiments has kept me on this. I think by giving this away I have gained it."

Douglas said I was stuck on wanting a particular experience, whether blissful or frightful, rather than seeing what was apparent. It was true that I expected enlightenment would hit me like an avalanche and be traumatic like Rose's experience. An even deeper belief was the expectation that the ultimate Truth would be undeniable. It must carry utter conviction. I had sought that certainty for years. If I had to convince myself of enlightenment's validity, then it was no better than any other belief.

My chief concern with Douglas' experience was the sheer ordinariness of it. Douglas touted that ordinariness, but followed by saying one's determination, passion, and trusting dictated whether they stuck with the seeing. Douglas did not think there were depths to the seeing, but some people were more trusting and more giving of themselves to the experience than others.

"Looking," Douglas said, "is consciousness turning upon itself. God self-aware courtesy of Shawn. While it seems the only way this happens is by a third-person consciousness doing something to see the first-person consciousness, this is only a working hypothesis. It seems that way, but it is not really so."

"Does this 'third-person' get in the way of consciousness?" I asked. By that, I meant do we have to do something, to change, evolve, or work on ourselves to overcome some mental obstacle?

"I might say it does in a way, but I try not to get too complicated. I try to stick to this [pointing at his face]."

Douglas dryly noted that I asked a lot of questions. He thought it good to doubt and question everything, but questioning was often a form of procrastination. Questions were the dragon that guarded the pearl of wisdom. It was better to act; to do the experiments and see. "I think the more we focus on the seeing, the more these big metaphysical questions we bellyache about will either be answered non-verbally or cease to be of importance to us."

He added, "We all dither, instead of being resolute in our handing over to seeing."

Despite my mind's continual objections, the moments of seeing without doubt lengthened as the week progressed. Especially clear to me was Douglas' insistence that, "We are built at center to give our lives for others." While some interpreted this as an excuse for hugging and brotherly love, I tended toward the neutral tones that Douglas emphasized. It simply seemed that whenever I faced another person, they were the only one there. They entered into an awareness, and action took place in that awareness. My awareness, which was not really "mine," was filled with others. Whether I could maintain this seeing in a situation like the New Mexico campground remained to be discovered.

There were ineffable moments with Douglas. People who spend their lives in service to truth charge the air around them. Douglas' home was near a church, and one morning he casually remarked as the bell tolled, "That's a medieval bell in a medieval church. There's a lot of history here. I think that's helpful. It is a sense of your roots. If you take a plant from Japan and plant it here, it won't grow as well. Important for the human, I mean. Your essence is already home. It probably doesn't matter for your essence."

The striking of a bell became a Zen sword, which became words with which Douglas sliced the ordinary moment and laid bare my longing for an ineffable "home."

Later that day I wrote, "As I gaze out at a medieval church viewed from the patio of Douglas' home, the peace of evening settles over my world. Birds feed in the lawn, there is singing in the trees. The abbot sips a cup of tea and chats about the weather. This seeing *is* a way home. It is a way to die before you die."

In another moment reminiscent of Rose, I asked Douglas if when he first "saw" he was convinced of its validity. He simply said, "Yes," and the authority and certainty in his voice silenced my questioning. Douglas' conviction was deep. When he spoke, his words carried me with him. Sometimes he spoke as passionately as a young man and at other times his voice was that of the nothingness quietly calling out to me.

There were frightening moments as well. Often, I felt my sense of self slipping away as if someone took the core out of me. There was an implication to Douglas' work that left me feeling something was deeply wrong—that same feeling I briefly sensed in isolation while on Rose's farm. What I thought most certain about me was terribly mistaken. That sick feeling was replaced at times by a simple awareness and direct seeing that I was not my mind or body. This seeing faded in and out, though, and I wondered how it would fare in the real world.

On my last day, Douglas asked, "Are you going to look for a job?"

It was an unexpected question. "Well, yes," I stammered.

"That's good. I think that's a good idea."

"Why do you say that?"

"Well, it's just a little suspicion. I think it's good to get out and meet people you wouldn't otherwise."

"The best is in this face to face meeting," he said. "You are always meeting people. Are you going to meet them like this [he butts his two fists together], or like this [his open palm meets his closed fist]? It's a constant reminder to see who you really are. Of course, you're always welcome here and there are friends in the States, and you can always share this with others. This though [again meeting his closed fist with an open palm], I think that is the real secret to keeping this up."

I left Douglas and the village of Nacton unconvinced of the solidity of the "seeing," but riding a bubble of inspiration. I glimpsed the beauty and wonder of my fellow humans and practiced looking just as he suggested. Yet within a few days of my return to the States, this equanimity crumbled when faced with the habits of my life. While the world looked beautiful from a distance, up close the oddities of my fellow humans, especially the ones I was closest to, proved a daunting challenge. Living the seeing outside Douglas' haven was a struggle. "Are you going to practice, or let it die?" I asked myself.

Chapter 14:
No Flip Side to the Coin

A person seeks with his whole being, which gets him nowhere.
Giving up gets him nowhere. He seeks for the sake of seeking;
not because of success or failure.

—Richard Rose

The short answer was, "I let it die." Away from Douglas, the experience of Headlessness faded. Though it
shook my assumptions, this was not enough to perma-
nently alter the core belief that I was a body and mind
separate from the world. Like that moment in the grove of
trees my freshman year of college, Headlessness became
one of a succession of glimpses of an alternate reality.
Despite these glimpses, I always returned to the familiar
ground of "me"—the feeling that I existed as a discrete,
independent entity separate from the world, an entity that
faced the world as a closed fist to a closed fist.

I pressed on with the geographic cure, and the end
of the year found me camped on the outskirts of Austin,

Texas, planning my conquest. Belle, LOC, the Farm, SKS, and Kentucky were now behind me—dead end after dead end. Even my fatigue was cast off. A year after starting cabergoline, my pituitary tumor was smaller and my testosterone and prolactin levels were normal. As if reborn, I was ready to tackle the world.

A fast-talking, hard-driving businessman named Lenny welcomed me to Austin and offered a step up from the campground. Lenny was an old TAT member, and though there was no secret TAT handshake, I instantly felt a kinship. He dealt in foreclosed homes, and I followed his directions down a dusty gravel road and past an algae-covered pond to one of his long vacant properties. The house looked as faded and abandoned as the surrounding land: there was no water, no phone, and no furniture. Flushing the toilet required a bucketful of pond water. I didn't care and happily threw my sleeping pad and bag on the hardwood floor. Later that night, something big and wild shuffled and squeaked under the floorboards. Whatever it was, I reasoned it could stay under the house as long as it left me the upstairs.

Bathing in pond water before a job interview was a bad idea, so I snuck into the campground shower and emerged as a clean-cut and earnest job seeker. Austin's economy was booming and offered an astonishing variety of jobs, but memories of Augie once again led me towards sales. Parked on the side of Interstate-35, an impromptu phone interview forced me to cover my lack of sales experience with enthusiasm. In a flash of intuition I blurted out, "I just really want to make a lot of money!" I started two days later. The job was straight commission—hawking custom closet renovations for an outfit called The Closet Factory—so no sales equaled no pay.

From campground, to empty house, to apartment in town, my hopeful evolution towards titan of business began. Armed with a munchkin-sized model of a premium closet replete with full-slide drawers, European hinges, chrome closet rods and medium-density fiberboard shelves, I drove from appointment to appointment giving free estimates. My task? To convince people to transform their closet from a cluttered box into a serenely organized, beautiful, and time-saving addition to their home (and to communicate that with sincerity). Other than the munchkin model, I didn't have much in my favor. My severely limited sales knowledge consisted of Augie's stories and a couple of books. "Inside of you is a model of every person you will ever sell to," one of them said. I held to that bit of wisdom like a mantra.

The closet design business was strangely intimate. Most appointments were with women surprised to find a man on their doorstep and generally hesitant to show me their closets. An embarrassing explosion of shoes, dresses, shirts, pants, skirts, hats, scarves, coats, and assorted other items greeted me at nearly every home. As I knelt on the floor to take a measurement, I noticed clothes that were likely unworn for months squeezed into every crevice.

People had too much shit, for certain. Yet that was the pain point I offered to alleviate—let me help you restore order to the chaos of useless belongings.

Many clients needed a personal organizer more than thousands of dollars of closet rehab, but I plunged ahead extolling our benefits. Our materials were well-made, and I excelled at measuring spaces and maximizing their use. By a stroke of luck there was a big sale my first month. "Don't want to buy today? Well, you should because the sale ends soon," I said and people bought! I was the top-selling designer for November. In two months I earned as much as I did in an entire year at LOC.

While I scrambled to succeed in sales, a part of me did not give a damn. After work, my nights were free to do whatever I pleased. Though the exuberance of meeting Douglas was over, and I was not meditating or writing po-etry, I felt the supreme value of the spiritual search. I took a chance on the spiritual journey and failed, but did not regret the effort. If nothing else, my psychological health had improved. I was more at ease in the world because of, rather than despite, knowledge of my ignorance. I had no great truths to share, but had met numerous interesting teachers in person or through books, as well as some ques-tionable characters. Austin was in the midst of the internet boom, and every service imaginable was migrating to the web. If someone could sell pet supplies and groceries from a website, then why couldn't I build a site that rated teachers? Spiritualteachers.org was thus born—the perfect

message-in-a-bottle to travel the world and share teachers
and books of value.

I began unearthing old notes, unpacking dusty
books, and digging deeper into teachers I had encountered. Franklin Merrell-Wolff was a good example. Mr.
Rose felt Merrell-Wolff was enlightened, but despite this
endorsement I never made it past the first few pages of
his densely worded *Experience and Philosophy*. I needed a
dictionary just to read the book's back cover:

> I found myself in sight of the limits to which
> our present egoistic consciousness has reached,
> and also had found adumbrations of another
> kind of consciousness where alone, it seemed,
> solution of the antinomies of the subject-object
> consciousness could be found.

Merrell-Wolff was dead, so I couldn't ask for elab-
oration, but a website offered transcripts of his lectures.
Hoping he spoke more simply than he wrote, I ordered
several and looked forward to their arrival.

The excitement of working on the website each
evening was a new feeling. It was a pleasure rather than
an obligation, like finding the gift you know a friend
will love. The desire arose without effort, will power, or
thought of reward. I seemed relieved, as well, of comparing my spiritual accomplishments to those of others. I was
no longer chasing enlightenment, and just hoped others

would learn from my successes, mistakes, and failures. Rather than helping because that was part of Rose's Law of the Ladder, I helped as a selfless offer of friendship. It was my message of hope to those who wandered in search of an answer.

Feeling inspired, I wrote this homage to Zen Master Huang Po:

> Beyond rightness
> What is reality?
> The mind grasps perfection,
> But what is an Eternity?
> Beyond the balance of life and death,
> Beyond the mind, bursting thought,
> "Nothing to cling to or stay your fall."

I knew the language and mood of the transcendent, but was still bound to this world's mysterious see-saw of life and death.

Nine days later, a package arrived from the Merrell-Wolff group. Excitedly opening it, I settled into reading the transcript of a talk titled "The Induction." Alone in my apartment on a Tuesday evening, Merrell-Wolff's long-dead words came alive and forever changed my life.

"Let's start a little analysis," Merrell-Wolff began, like a friend stepping beside me to share some playful thought.

He began a self-analysis, a deconstruction of the self, actually; first addressing the body.

"So we come to the first stage of self-analysis. It runs generally this way: I ask, 'What am I?' And first it occurs to me that the idea that I am this body is a delusion, because this body is an object before my consciousness. I speak as though it were my body, I speak as though I possess it. It is therefore external to me. I am not the body."

I agreed, what I saw was not me; the view was not the viewer.

Next, Merrell-Wolff addressed the roaring rage of our feelings.

"Are those feelings of I? No, for I experience them. I but experience them. They are different from me. I can identify them, and that itself is enough proof that they are not I."

I agreed, again. I saw "my" feelings as a thing apart; occurring outside of my sense of I-ness. I had noticed this for many years.

Next, he broached thought.

"Am I this body of thoughts in my mind? No. One gets a little closer to his thoughts than to anything else, and it's a little harder to untangle this. But if he watches and studies closely enough, the thoughts come to me."

This, too, I saw occurring time and again in meditation. Thoughts entered my mind without effort on my part.

Having dissected the body, feelings, and thoughts, Merrell-Wolff pointed to the last bastion of identity.

"I'm not the mind, I'm not the feelings, I'm not the body—that I see. But I surely am, I surely am an individual, apart from others."

This was my sense of identity; the sense I existed in this world.

"Now what you've gotten a hold of is a very difficult fellow—it's your ego. He can sneak around and confuse you like the dickens. You can spend years trying to get behind him."

Which I had. My meditations tried and tried to see beyond the black wall in my mind.

"And what you do, you can get into an infinite regression. You look at your ego. All right, here am I and all of a sudden it dawns upon you that which is looking at the ego is really the I. So you stick that one out in front. You look at it again, but then you realize it couldn't be, because here is a something that is observable."

Yes, the infinite regression; my mind spinning round and round; the noting of noting in Vipassana; awareness watching awareness and finding no resolution to this conundrum.

"At last it finally dawns that I AM THAT which is never an object before Consciousness. And mayhap, at that moment, in your analysis—the Heavens will open."

As these words entered my mind the room filled with energy, like rapport, like that long-ago moment by the student center under the pine trees, but with the intensity of an engulfing flame. Tears erupted, poured down my face, and obscured the room. Merrell-Wolff's words were true; literally, physically true. I, Shawn, was ever an object, and ever a thing destined to die. It was obvious and undeniable that I was and always would be doomed to die. In the face of that stark realization, I felt my self fading away, but there was no fight. I did not run from death because there was nowhere to run. The runner himself was vanishing, and as that happened something became startlingly clear—the nothingness that I was fading into and had so feared was already inside me. Outside and inside were fundamentally the same. How could this be? How could there be only one thing? No observer, no observed, just ONE.

This implosive realization gripped my head like a vice and forced me to the floor. I was being consumed by something too vast for the mind to hold. I felt I was dying, but I was not afraid.

Two or three times the pain lessened and I climbed back to the chair, but it came again and again I fell to the floor. Lines from Richard Rose's "Three Books of the Absolute," appeared in my mind: "O eternal spaces, art thou black or white… Is thy form clothed in light or darkness?" Over and over I answered, "No, No, It IS. There is not black or white."

The mind could not contain the merging of two into one, and the gut-level, crushing feeling that one is equivalent to *none*. With no observer, there was nothing to observe and nothing to be observed. The feeling was of slipping into darkness, losing all I had held to so tightly, losing words, images, thoughts, and feeling. Going to sleep yet finding I was still awake, but not as an "I." Instead there existed only the still, silent blackness that is sleep. A blackness that was motionless yet vibrant. Dark yet shimmering. Silent yet vibrating. Dead yet potent. Suddenly, the agony culminated. No words remained. Only THIS.

Silence in a space without bounds. A self with no container, containing nothing, contained by nothing.

A voice appeared in this silence, saying "Not this way." As if reemerging, or reentering, or realizing suddenly I was in a room, objects appeared. In my journal, I scrawled these words:

God is here. He rings in the death of all we know.
Rejoice, the end begins.
A new life. Nothing ever the same.
We are everlasting.
Rejoice. I am free. Behind these words flows everlasting Light.
It's back there. Doors open. Look inside.
This is my way. No plan.
You cannot follow, but you must try.
God is here. God IS HERE now.

The sobbing waned. I was stunned, shell-shocked. Somehow I found my way to bed and fell into a deep sleep.

The next morning I woke up and went to work. Rather than leave home for a cave as the great Indian teacher Ramana Maharshi did, habit moved me out the door and to my car. I felt a half-step away from my body and mind, like a robot watching its programming execute, but the quality of experience was not cold and sterile. On the contrary, everything was perfect and effortless. My job helping people create more space in their closets to pack with more stuff seemed ludicrous, however. I told my first client they did not need our system and should just clean out their closets. There was no interest in convincing people to buy if they were uncertain.

The evening after this experience, I scribbled a few more journal entries. I remarked that John Davis was right when he said, "A man's task is to go into the abyss, and come out with something."[5] However, this *something* was not added to me, rather all was subtracted from me and what remained was the truth. "It's nothing and it's everlasting," I wrote. "Beauty which the mind cannot conceive. It is the end of everything dual/mundane/sensory. And that's fine. The end of our life doesn't matter. Reality always IS. It's there always."

This was more than awareness. Awareness was bound to the body, "To identify one's self with aware-

---

5   *See* www.spiritualteachers.org/john_davis.htm.

ness, to say 'Oh, yeah, there is something that watches my thinking and is always there,' does not answer the question of immortality. I claim that is an intellectual understanding. The experience, to become that awareness, that 'I-less' awareness even for a moment will knock you to the floor. It is more than the mind can grasp."

Two days later I wrote, "When I pause in my thinking, a mild sense of unreality pervades this world. My head still aches and the experience still rests just below my thoughts. The feeling of All-ness rests there. I'm still alive. I've marveled at that several times today. There is still a body which went to work, ate, showered, and such. It is good that habits are established because that is the only thing keeping the body moving."

The certainty I found lacking in my reaction to Douglas' experiments was now everywhere I looked: "This wasn't like 'seeing' in the sense of what occurred while practicing with Douglas. While the seeing itself was experiential, it was so light in its touch that it required the intellect for support. An attitude of, 'Oh yeah, I see what you mean. That must mean I have no head.' Plunging into that dark silence was not willful. There was no decision in what happened to me. It happened like a piano falling. I became All."

I could not live in the Absolute, however. By its very definition it was all-absorbing, and there was no functioning when there were no pairs of opposites. Equally true was that the mind, a product of duality, could forget. I understood how Rose could be mumbling in a nursing home, and how memory didn't matter because the mind was not real. We didn't take our personality with us. The personality was nothing compared to what IS. Maybe our personality was like a drop in the ocean, but who cared for that drop when we were really the Ocean?

At last I knew there was a Final Answer. There was an end to life that was not oblivion. It was an alive Void. It was utter Completeness. I had no idea if it mattered that the mind realized this. No idea if there were other lives, bardos, or universes. All I knew was that my particular spiritual hunger was answered.

As days passed, I dissected my memories to create a story of what happened, but the story made little sense. How could I have a memory of Nothing? I went to the edge of death and maintained a sense of a body lying on a floor at least until the culmination, at which point there was Nothing. There was a memory of this Nothing, which seemed impossible unless the mind was present... which it couldn't be. My best explanation was it's like standing next to the ocean. There's a feel to that experience and the mind has a reaction to it. Now imagine the mind is a sand castle on the beach. A wave rolls in and pulls down the castle. The mind has a reaction to this, even as it is pulled apart. The wave recedes, the castle reassembles itself, yet each grain is marked from being submerged in the ocean. What's left is memory that elicits feelings akin to the last moments of duality, and a mind that knows the taste of the ocean, and hears the waves. I would not want to go through the dissolution again. It was agony. I glimpsed Reality and that was enough.

Now about that agony. Though this quality was similar to Rose's description, I don't think that was a hallmark of enlightenment. Rather, I had a big ego, a very strong sense of self, so more explosive was needed. The agony was linked to how tightly the mind was held together. I understood why Saul fell from his horse on the road to Damascus, but I suspected that some left behind their self with less trauma.

Unlike Saul, I was not instantly transformed into a saint. I still slept and dreamed. I still liked pop-tarts and sunny days. The ego, I, awareness, observer, self, attention, all these pieces of me still existed, but were of the same insubstantial cloth of experience. I now understood cosmic consciousness and how there was still an ego, still an "I," in that experience. That consciousness might be infinitely expanded, but there was always a sense of self at the center of that boundlessness. There must be in order to live in this world. The final reality was not "I am All," rather the final reality was "All" stripped of any ownership.

Though not a saint, I was much less concerned with the world. Except for the desire to communicate this to people. To communicate that there was an End. There was Certainty. You could know something for sure. "There is a place," I said, "which is no-place, where there is no flip side to the coin."

A month later, driving thirty-five miles per hour on a busy thoroughfare, a woman made an illegal left turn in front of me. My foot slammed the brakes, and I instinctively yelled—the ancient, guttural scream of a warrior charging into battle. The brakes did nothing, and I heard no sound as my body absorbed the impact of striking the side of her car. Eyeglasses launched off my face, the world blurred, then all was still. I grabbed the glasses from the dash and leapt out of the seat. A rivulet of bright-green fluid crept from under the car. My knee was sore. An ambulance arrived. I sat on the curb watching as they hauled out the other driver strapped to a backboard. I shook my head in disbelief as the EMT taped an ice pack to my knee. I was not floating above the scene, nor did I smile beatifically as I crashed. I didn't even know how to get home until the tow truck driver offered me a lift. Enlightenment had not graced me with superhuman powers.

My car was totaled, so I bought a small, white truck. Within a week, I pulled in front of a Ford Mustang which crushed the driver's side door. Accident-free for fourteen years, I became convinced I had to leave Austin or die. I quit my job and made the long arc back through Colorado and across the plains to Kentucky—essentially retracing the prior year's journey. A strange, rootless feeling nagged me. I felt at once completely at ease, yet unmoored and without the slightest sense of what to do next. The only thought was to return to my old home at the Linsly Outdoor Center. It was a refuge after leaving the Farm and would be so again.

At some point on the road to LOC, I attempted to summarize the past nine years of search:

> From college through grad school's first year,
> I drifted in insecurity and illusion. The SKS
> restored me to a relatively well-functioning,
> adjusted human being; a man of good character
> with an interest in spiritual matters. Isolation
> time and Richard Rose drove me to look at
> my mind and discover the source of thought. I
> broke my hammer on that wall. Douglas Hard-
> ing gave me a new, bigger hammer and I began
> to see Light. Nine years of search, perhaps, led
> me to the propitious moment where life ended,
> and All took its place.

Truly, I returned home a changed man.

Epilogue

*Your brain thinks it knows what **nothing** is. Thinks it knows what it is to BE nothing. Thinks it knows what it is to disappear. But that's precisely what the brain doesn't know.*

—s.n.

The Sanskrit to English translation of Nirvana is "blowing out" or "extinguished," and when I first heard that definition I felt an instant recognition of the term. That is precisely what happens. The self is extinguished and something non-personal remains. There are no words to describe it, as this cannot be conceived by the mind.

Everywhere I look the trees and hillsides are painted on a backdrop of stillness. This stillness immediately calls forth the same feeling of stillness inside me. Motion and stillness, life and death, are interwoven and the beauty of transience, the beauty of momentary action upon an eternal screen stirs me to tears. "I've seen things you people wouldn't believe," says the dying Roy Batty at the closing of *Blade Runner*. "All those moments will be lost in time, like tears in rain." It is true from the perspective of the individual, but lost only by absorption into something greater and grander than our imagination.

Besides this stillness, the other change I notice is that the fundamental *dis-ease* with which I walked through the world is gone. No longer am I alone against the universe. I am certain of my place—both alone in and united with a universe that contains no bad or good. The question of meaning has evaporated. Only in my existential loneliness did I seek the comfort of meaning. Freed from that loneliness, meaning becomes a fabrication. Likewise, purpose, that brother of meaning, no longer has a use. Meaning and purpose are fanciful stories I told to support a vision of Shawn as an independent, long-lasting entity.

Life goes on after enlightenment, with all of its challenges, disappointments, discoveries, and triumphs. Maybe this book doesn't fit your view of enlightenment. Where is the permanent happiness? What is the practical benefit? How is life different? These are the sorts of questions one peering down the spiritual path may ask. Bernadette Roberts said that spiritual realization had nothing to do with this world, while Douglas Harding found it eminently practical. Richard Rose was not one to talk about the benefits of enlightenment, though he spoke in "Zen and Common Sense" that even if a person didn't achieve enlightenment, the search made sense:

>...the longer that you follow the self-confrontation, the self-analysis, the better off you are

to just live with yourself, and for other people to live with you… And you take a new broader view of things because your egos are not in the way, destroying your friendships, and destroying your family, your financial possibilities even.[6]

Others in the spiritual community dispute that there is even such a thing as enlightenment. One nonduality teacher criticized TAT for holding up enlightenment as the end of the spiritual path. "They say certain people are enlightened and that means they are done," he said. "What does that mean? Done like a baked potato?" Instead of enlightenment as an end point, some espouse it as the beginning of a continual evolution of consciousness.

It does not matter one whit whether enlightenment is sudden or gradual, an end point or just the beginning. What matters is that you begin to search. The danger lies in dismissing the idea of enlightenment because it doesn't fit your preconception, or in procrastinating by endlessly comparing descriptions. In that case, logic hides the deep desire for truth that is in your heart.

From my perspective, enlightenment has nothing to do with this world, this body, brain, or person, yet it is eminently preferable to the alternative of uncertainty. On the practical side, the desperation and longing that

6   *See* www.searchwithin.org/download/zen_and_common_sense.pdf.

drove my life are gone. Rather than being driven, I am being discovered. Life is unrolling before me. That leaves me open to surprising actions and reactions. Depending on my mood, life is a grand struggle, a mystery, a pain in the ass, or perfection. Contentedness pervades my life, yet I get angry, depressed, frustrated, and tired. How could this be? I am aware of the air itself, and realize that both positive and negative feelings are breezes—ripples on a pond that always returns to stillness.

At turns frustrating and fascinating, it is clear that the evolution of the expression of enlightenment in this body will go on till my dying day. Though the center is at rest, the wheel does not stop turning. I am both the hub, the spoke and the rim. As long as I stand on this planet the wheel keeps spinning.

As I walk onto the deck this evening, a cool breeze blows, the lights of San Francisco shimmer in the distance, and a clear sky is space containing all below it. I am thankful I could never have imagined this. Being surprised is a fine way to live.

Life itself is like watching a pebble roll down a stream, silently colliding with other pebbles. The pebble's edges are rounding, smoothing, and bringing an ever increasing ease to the journey. Now and then a glint from the rippling water catches my eye, blinding me to all else but that flash of light. A light so bright it brings darkness.

Enlightenment—such a big, crazy, mixed-up word. It is just a word. What matters is the desire in your heart for the truth. That desire will guide you as far as you need to go, but it is not easy to hear the heart and then take action. Such action is the work we must do to follow the spiritual path.

Perhaps you think me crazy, or a liar, or suffering from a brain tumor (which I am!). It does not matter if you discount me. Just do not use that as an excuse to discount the search itself. Although you must ultimately go it alone, there are others who have found the Truth. Find some voice that appeals to you and follow it. If awakening can happen to me, it can happen to anyone. I, and others, elevated Richard Rose to status of a superman and thought we could never be as hungry, determined, truthful, or dedicated as him. Yet, he said anyone of average intelligence could attain this. I am proof that is true.

These are just words, playing like a song
in a room quickly emptying.

Spiritual First Aid

The main obstacle to success is that people don't start,
the second is that they don't persist,
the third is they don't adapt.

—*s.n.*

Now that the story has been told, I want to leave you with a few words of advice. Fundamentally, the spiritual path I've outlined is a *Way of Subtraction*—a peeling away of all we are not in order to discover what we are. While there is no step-by-step guide to enlightenment, what I will offer you are basic principles to apply and adapt as needed. Think of these as spiritual first aid.

The core principle is to…

1. Practice honesty:

Richard Rose said the way to Truth was to "back away from untruth." To postulate the Truth is to lie to ourselves. Instead, recognize what is untrue and turn away from it. This is *neti, neti*—rejecting what we are not in order to discover what we are.

Begin by developing self-honesty in ordinary life. Learn to identify your daily lies, as this translates to seeing the larger ones. Recognize conflicting desires in your mind and how each of these voices makes the others seem untrue. Listen to the one that feels most truthful and work with that best guess until you discover a better one.

It is easy to rationalize dishonesty, especially when your self-image is assailed. Books, being in nature, music, meditation, and meaningful conversations with friends may give you a truer perspective. A worthy spiritual teacher helps with identifying your lies. Around them, you may sense their perspective and glimpse the self-created fabric of your daily dramas.

Group self-inquiry or confrontation is a synthetic catalyst for honesty. Find a group of people, in person or online, with whom you can engage in honest dialogue and questioning to understand the assumptions and beliefs that power many of your thoughts.

As you practice honesty, it will make it easier to…

2. Remember your natural koan:

Within each of us is a question that demands an answer. "Why am I miserable?" "What is love?" "How can I find peace?" "Is there life after death?" "What is the purpose of life?" "Am I awake or dreaming?" "Who am I?" "What am I?" "What do I really want?" "Why am I here?" "What is thought?" "Where does thought come from?" "What is Real?" "What lasts?" These are just a few natural koans. Every seeker must discover and then find ways to remember their natural koan. Do not pursue a question because, "I think I *should* be asking it." If "Who is the thinker?" is a meaningless question to you, then drop it and find a question that makes you ache for an answer.

If your natural koan is not obvious, sit alone and write down the questions that concern you. Look for one that feels most important and imagine the feeling of finding an answer. Begin work on your question with whatever offers ways and means of discovery. Beginning is more important than waiting till you know the "right" way to begin.

Any question, pursued with the idea of arriving at complete certainty regarding the answer, will lead to a spiritual realization. Unearthing the determination to follow the question to its end is the hard part. Do not be surprised if your koan changes over time. This is actually a sign of deepening practice.

I found the questions easy to discover, but remembering them was hard. There were times it seemed all of life was trying to distract and lull me into forgetfulness. Making time to remember my natural koan fed the determination and led me ever deeper inside.

Some teachers say to simply drop the search and free yourself from this bothersome desire for answers. If you could you would, but the process does not work that way. You can give up, but all that will happen is you become a person who gives up. Instead, harness your desire and it becomes the stick that stirs the fire of self inquiry while simultaneously being consumed.[7]

Now that you remember your natural koan…

3. Focus your energy:

The spiritual path is no different from other endeavors in life: apply energy and you will see results. To build focus, read from a spiritually themed book before going to sleep. Your last thoughts before sleep influence your dreams. Set a problem before your mind and a solution may appear during the night. Forgo the news at breakfast and read a book, listen to inspiring music, or practice mindful eating.[8] While commuting, listen to lectures, or ride in silence. Douglas Harding has a meditation for driving that gives insight into one's true nature.[9]

---

7   "Since every other thought can occur only after the rise of the 'I'-thought and since the mind is nothing but a bundle of thoughts, it is only through the enquiry 'Who am I?' that the mind subsides. Moreover, the integral 'I'-thought, implicit in such enquiry, having destroyed all other thoughts, gets itself finally destroyed or consumed, just as the stick used for stirring the burning funeral pyre gets consumed. " ~ from the essay "Who Am I," *The Collected Works of Ramana Maharshi*.

8   See Joseph Goldstein's *The Experience of Insight*.

9   Douglas Harding, *Face to No-Face*, Inner Directions Publishing, 2000, pp. 23-25.

Curtail daydreaming with a mantra or prayer. I took to heart Richard Rose's advice to think of nothing rather than tolerate rambling thoughts and would count from one to ten, over and over, until the daydreams receded.

Skip lunchtime gossip and find a quiet place to break the work or school state of mind. Get fresh air and remind your self what is truly important.

Turn your social instinct towards finding spiritual friends. Discuss your feelings or latest endeavors, rather than talk about sports or work. Ask why you feel the need to talk. Do you really have something to contribute, or are you burning off nervous energy that could be channeled to your ultimate goal?

Let your exercise time double as self-observation. Notice when your body wants to stop exercising, how if you keep pushing the body goes along with your desire, and how that same pattern of action and resistance applies in other areas of your life. Simply watching the muscles move is amazing. Try to determine when you consciously move a muscle. Where did the thought to raise your arm originate? Who decided when your arm would stop moving? Watch closely.

If watching tv or a movie, pick something thought-provoking rather than completely escapist. Recall Richard Rose's confrontational adage that, "If you need entertainment, you are asleep."

Use meals to test the effects of different foods upon your thinking or your energy level. Make a game of observing people. Test your intuition about what people will do or say. Practice awareness of your thoughts and look for their cause and origin. Notice and remember the results of your experiments. Keep a notepad handy to record your observations and inspirations.

These cumulative actions build a vector and forge a direction for your life, but as soon as you commit to one thing, a dozen other desires clamor for your attention. Identify and reduce the many obsessions that draw your attention in other directions and prevent any real achievement.

Keep a daily log of how you spend your time during a week. Brainstorm a number of categories such as: travel, entertainment, food, socializing, work, housekeeping, daydreaming, sleep, etc. Write down your weekly time estimate for each category. Comparing this with the actual numbers indicates how observant and/or honest you are regarding your actions. See what percentage of time is spent in each category, then set goals for how you would like that to change.

Now that you are focusing your energy, realize that you must...

4. Fall and rise a thousand times if need be:

Experience difficulty completing the daily time log? Congratulations, you just uncovered a major stumbling block to achievement. To overcome this block, try the exercise again. Determine to keep trying until you record a week of data. Do not berate yourself if you fail repeatedly. Muster a dogged, humble determination.

Change is accomplished in little steps as well as leaps of inspiration. Do not ignore inspirations, but do not wait for them either. Little steps may be shaky, but the cumulative effect is strong. Even inspirations need little steps for reinforcement.

Mr. Rose once said, "If I tell you to go five miles, don't walk a mile, then turn back." Though I certainly fell to the ground many times, I always got up and kept walking. Why? Because I knew in my heart that there was *nothing else to do.*

While you wipe the dust off your pants, remember to...

5. Identify and, if necessary, repair patterns:

As a society, we learn the patterns of biology, chemistry, and physics to gain control of our environment. Yet, the patterns in our internal environment draw little attention.

Faced with a difficult task, my first reaction is to throw up my hands in despair. I get depressed at the thought of quitting and equally depressed at the thought of trying and failing. After wallowing in futility, an idea appears and I start to work. By recognizing this pattern rather than being completely absorbed in it, the power of the despair lessens. Observation helps the mechanism self-repair by interrupting the chain of thoughts that binds it to the pattern. Less energy is wasted, and I even see a bit of humor in the mind being up to its old tricks. The pattern speeds up—the time between despair and effort decreases—and eventually comes close to vanishing.

Keeping a journal helps you identify patterns and ruts, reminds you of inspirations, and provides another perspective from which to examine your thoughts and feelings. Study how you react to trauma and stress. Study the patterns in your friends and realize you are no different. Make notes of thoughts you have around certain people, places, or situations.

You will not like some patterns: habits learned from your parents, lusts and fears, greed, envy, pride, and an array of neuroses. A natural reaction is to set about repairing these patterns. However, there is no need to become a saint or an expert mechanic of the psyche, nor will the gates of heaven open because of your good behavior. Do not waste precious time sculpting the nuances of your personality to conform to standards whose origin are buried in unexamined beliefs and assumptions.

The opposite approach is to observe and let any thought and action take place—claim the philosophic stance that the observer is unaffected by anything it observes. The victims of your pseudo-detached rampage will disagree.

Some personality facets must change while others need not. Change that which slows your ability to practice honesty, remember your koan, focus your energy, or any of the other spiritual first aid items. Some will change through observation, while others require additional help.

For example, if you are afraid to speak to people, then your ability to help and be helped by others is hindered. To change, keep observing the trait in action, delve into its origin, throw your self again and again into the challenging situation, laugh at the whole ridiculous process, and keep trying. Eventually, you become a person who speaks when needed. It may never be pleasant, but when the need arises you act. A total cure is not required; only enough to keep moving on the quest.

On the other hand, if you are afraid to speak to people who own black cats, you may be occasionally inconvenienced in daily life, and irritated or embarrassed by this seeming defect, but it is not worth the investment of precious time and energy to unearth the causes and change the habit. Unless, of course, you stumble upon a spiritual teacher or potential spouse with a fondness for black cats.

As you work on identifying patterns, be sure to...

6. Develop intuition:

Intuition, along with reason, guides us through life. Intuition is the feeling, the hunch, and the faint whisper—often obscured by reasoned thought and not always correct. Intuition spans a continuum from feeling one should turn left instead of right, to knowing what another person is thinking, to a taste of the profound.

Intuition is tied to your interests. A football receiver pivots right rather than left, a dedicated gambler "knows" what card to play, while a therapist gets an insight about a patient. Focusing your energy helps your intuition. Here are other techniques that proved useful for me:

Observation of the mind: Watch the decision-making process in your mind, and learn to distinguish among the conflicting desires. Perhaps you have the intuition to eat a doughnut. Over time, you recognize that as an intuition of the body desiring sugar. You may recognize a higher intuition that says not to eat the doughnut and to take a walk instead. During your walk, an even higher intuition may be sensed, saying that neither doughnuts, nor walking, nor anything about you is of importance.

Prayer: This can be a statement of your intention to improve your intuition. There were times I asked whatever might be listening to help improve my intuition. The prayer is strengthened if accompanied by feeling. Feel the longing to improve your intuition, and try to recall an instance where you saw the intuition in action. The words of the prayer, plus the feeling, plus the memory are an arrow launched into the realm of possibility. Lastly, forget about it. Don't wait anxiously for the prayer's answer. Pray with all your heart, then let it go.

Another prayer involves listening for something other than the usual verbal barrage in our minds. Behind the verbal noise are other ways of knowing.

Creative endeavors: Writing, painting, music and other creative acts are helpful, especially if these are unusual activities for you. This develops your inner listening skills. If needed, read books or consult artists on how to begin such activities, but artistic technique is not a prerequisite. The process of watching your hand move over piano keys, for instance, letting the hand be guided by a feeling, letting the feeling move out of darkness and into life without hindering it—this is what matters.

Both creativity and prayer involve listening.[10] Sitting before a blank sheet of paper is a prayer. In its purest form, art is an attempt to discover the fount of creation. Allow the force of life/creation to manifest through your hand, or voice, or in whatever medium you work. The only power the self has is to block the light of life with the ego's shade. Because of this, moments of creation carry the sense of freedom from the ego.

Association with intuitive people: Discuss how they make decisions and how their mind functions. Those you associate with will change who you are.

Empathy development: This forces the use of feeling rather than logic. Take a job or volunteer in a helping profession. Work with children or the elderly—people who need your help and may have trouble communicating via words, forcing you to reach out with all of your senses to understand them.

---

10   See Bob Fergeson's *The Listening Attention* for more on this.

ESP Experiments: Practice telepathy, card reading, precognition, etc. Confirmation bias makes the mind prone to remember the results that match your hopes and expectations, so be scientific and record your results.

Natural settings: A walk in a park may stir the intuition. Being in nature gives a clearer perspective on our daily problems. It allows a relaxation of the survival instinct and creates space for thinking along new lines.

Celibacy: Practicing this clears distracting noise from the mind. If mental chatter associated with the pursuit of a mate is lessened, there are more resources available for observing the mind. Rose considered this the first step for improving the intuition.

Fasting: This slows the mental chatter, allowing observation of previously unknown mental territory. The mind literally becomes too tired to think, leaving you with…?

Dream work: Recording dreams and pondering their feel and meaning opens one to a different way of knowing. Related to this, Jim Burns advised people to fall asleep and wake up slowly.[11] The period between wake and sleep is fertile ground for all sorts of insights that appear to drop into the mind rather than result from logical thought.

These are just a few ideas. It takes a bit of intuition and reasoned experimentation to find methods of developing your intuition. It is trial and error. If you feel at a

---

11   Jim Burns, *At Home with the Inner Self*, TAT Foundation Press, 2011, pp. 49 and 114.

complete loss, then ask someone who is intuitive, or try anything just to take the first step and get moving. Many fears may stand between you and the intuition. The intuition might hint at a course of action for which the reason sees no call. Take the chance. Generally, all you stand to lose is false pride, although you will imagine it much more dangerous than that. Do not be afraid to follow the intuition, as it will grow if allowed.

Eventually, there is little else to guide you on the spiritual path except intuition. You follow a feeling that somewhere within you is the answer to your questions. You follow a feeling of the profound.

As you follow that feeling…

7. Be thankful:

Giving thanks acknowledges that you are not the center of the Universe and relinquishes some of your imaginary control of life. This thankfulness should be spontaneous rather than obligatory, though if you look for the urge to say "thank you" you may find a part of yourself stifling it. Give space for thanks.

Quietly acknowledge the fortune in your life. Let each word of thanks loosen your grip on life. With each small victory and each word of thanks, leave some of the self-will and be guided by Truth.

As you give thanks…

8. Look for the source:

This is turning inward to look for the source of thoughts, feeling, intuition, or "I-ness." Whatever you believe your-self to be, look to find where it originates. This approach starts with the proposition that anything observable is not us. "The view is not the viewer," Richard Rose said, though for years I did not grasp what he meant. However, I did understand that anything observable is not permanent, and what I wanted to know was what about me would not change and fade away—was there anything Real?

Looking for the source involves practicing honesty. I am not that cup of water on the table. I am not the hand typing this sentence. I am not these words appearing in my mind. I am not awareness. You can logically conclude this, but to experience it is totally different. You have to look inside your mind and see for yourself.

Again and again you search, rejecting every thought as not you, every sound or vision, and your sense of self even, because you see them all in your mind's eye. Yet, some *thing* turns away from all these objects—an awareness that is impossibly aware of itself and senses something else behind it. It tries to turn upon itself only to find itself. It—you—have come to the black wall.

The image of the black wall is indicative of what I sensed. It was an unknown around which my awareness pirouetted with itself—a desperate dance at the dead end street of the mind. You may explain the feeling with a different image—perhaps simply as fear, wonder, perplexity, or intense tension as if trying to grasp infinity or zero.

The method of rejecting what we see as not us, takes us directly to the fundamental uncertainty of our self knowledge. That fundamental uncertainty is masked by a fear of extinction which rises up when we get too close to the Truth. Your life of honesty and determination will carry you through this wall, through death, to Life.

Following are two quotes that strike at the heart of going within. They challenged and inspired me to keep looking:

> Am I this body of thoughts in my mind? No. One gets a little closer to his thoughts than to anything else, and it's a little harder to untangle this. But if he watches and studies closely enough, the thoughts come to me. I accept or reject them. That which accepts or rejects them is different from the thought. And then I finally reach this point where I find that I must be this something, in some sense, different from other people. I'm not the mind, I'm not the feelings, I'm not the body—that I see. But I surely *am*, I surely am an individual, apart from others.
>
> Now what you've gotten a hold of is a very difficult fellow—it's your ego. He can sneak around and confuse you like the dickens. You can spend years trying to get behind him.

And what you do, you can get into an infinite regression. You look at your ego. All right, here am I and all of a sudden it dawns upon you that *that* which is looking at the ego is really the I. So you stick that one out in front. You look at it again, but then you realize it couldn't be, because here is a something that is observable. At last it finally dawns that I AM THAT which is *never* an object before Consciousness. And mayhap, at that moment, in your analysis—the Heavens will open.

—Franklin Merrell-Wolff,
The Induction

From this point, as we look to the right, we notice that we can also look at awareness, and we can be aware of consciousness, and of looking at ourself looking indefinitely. We do not take a step forward, but are taken forward from here, by that which seems to be an accident, – an accident which does not come unless we have struggled relentlessly to find that which was unknown to us, by a method which could not be charted because the end or goal was unknown. We must have first become a vector. We must first have spent a good period of time studying our own awareness and consciousness

with our own consciousness until we acciden-
tally or by some unknown purpose, – enter the
source of our awareness.

—Richard Rose,
Psychology of the Observer

This looking at awareness, the infinite regression,
occurs as a rising and falling in time.
As an aid to your path…

9. Find a teacher(s):

A teacher is a friend with more experience on the spiritual
path. It may be a series of teachers—each giving you a tool
to use in your inner exploration. A book or audio record-
ing may be as important as a living person. Daily life is a
teacher, as well, if you take time to reflect on the lessons
without spinning the story to support your self-image.

We generally think of a teacher as a guru—someone
with an exalted position and air about them. Be aware of
looking for teachers that match your preconceptions of
what a spiritual path should be or how a teacher should
act. Be careful of teachers who want something from you
such as money, sex, or worship.

The best teachers will point you in a direction and
show you how to walk. Your job is to listen and apply
the teaching to your life. Learn by doing. Use their

methods, but adapt them to your personality. Franklin Merrell-Wolff said this well:

> In no case have I had any results that were worth the effort so long as I did not supply at least a self-devised modification of my own. Apparently the modification is suggested intuitively. Often I got results by a method diametrically opposite to that suggested by a given authority. At least, so far as my private experience is concerned, the successful method always had to be in some measure an original creation.[12]

When the opportunity arises to ask questions of a teacher, don't let shyness stop you. Ask questions about your self and not abstractions about the nature of the Absolute, God, and Heaven. These big questions are best explained in silence. Put down the pen when it is time to be silent and just feel. Share your successes and failures and be willing to expose your ignorance.

At times, you will grow angry and critical of your teacher. Study this. Your anger is frustration with your limited life, your lack of progress, and your lack of earnestness. Your criticism is your habitual way of life attempting to preserve itself—your ego fearing change.

Do not let the teacher's advice overrule what you feel in your heart. You may discover you were wrong, but that

---

12   Franklin Merrell-Wolff, *Experience and Philosophy*, 1994, p. 117.

is the only way to develop the ability to find your path. That you *must* do, for the teacher cannot lead you all the way.

In the quest for a teacher, be aware of the tendency to jump from teacher to teacher, looking for the next-greatest-thing, or jumping ship at the first sign of your inspiration lessening.

Do not rely on just a teacher, for you must…

10. Help and be helped:

"You are the average of the five people you spend the most time with," says Jim Rohn. There is tremendous benefit from associating with like-minded people, as it provides the matrix for helping and being helped which Richard Rose described in his Law of the Ladder.[13] Those on rungs below yours give a push, and those above give a pull. Reach too far down the ladder, and you will be pulled down, but reach too far up, and you will not understand how to work with that person.

Because each spiritual path is unique, it is difficult to work with a group. Groups tend to either homogenize and become cult-like, or break apart. However, if the majority of members are sincerely seeking (looking within), this enables diversity and understanding.

To amplify group work, share an apartment or house with a group of seekers. This is a resource of ideas and

---

13   Richard Rose, *The Albigen Papers*, Third Edition, 1978, pp. 199-201.

inspiration, as well as aid with the everyday problems of life. You learn from each other's successes and failures. When one member is in despair, his fellows carry him until he recovers.

The ego hinders us from reaching out to others. We fear looking foolish, making a mistake, or being rejected. Or the ego twists the desire to be of service into a wish to control, dominate, and be powerful.

With persistent self-honesty, true compassion develops—you see your flaws in others and their flaws in you. Discover that you actually *want* to be of service. This is different than the "enlightened self interest" of helping others because it will help you in the long run. You suffered through roadblocks and dry spells, and you want to help others in a similar situation. Ironically, your selfish time spent in self-study eventually allows you to operate selflessly.

Another bit of seeming selfishness that pays dividends is to...

11. Spend time alone:

People have ventured into deserts, forests, mountains, and caves for thousands of years to escape their fellows, find peace, and find answers to their deepest questions. These days, a person may camp out, get a cheap motel room, go to a fancy retreat center, or even hide in their room. Ideally, such time is an undistracted attempt to delve within in search of the truth of your being. However, it may become an escape into daydream and fantasy. For me, a few days or weeks alone each year allowed a clearer perspective on the rest of my life and was a time to pursue meditation with full intensity. What follows are some suggestions for the process.

First, you need a reason for your isolation—a topic, goal, or practice you want to explore. Many people take a few minutes in the morning or evening to review and plan for the coming day. Isolation is an opportunity to review and plan for months or years of your life. In my isolations I sometimes reviewed my journals from the past year. This was a priceless opportunity to see how I changed, how I spent or wasted time, and what my actions said about my priorities. I learned from history.

You can use isolation for reviewing and planning or for creating and discovering. Think about the scientist working late at night in his lab, the artist in their retreat, or the Native American on a vision quest. This is eliminating distractions so one can look within and see what arises. For a moment, put the demands of society on hold. No cell phones, no bills to pay, and no class or job to attend. Just you and the universe—you and life at its simplest.

Once you realize a reason for isolation, the question becomes how long? I spent anywhere from a half a day to thirty days in isolation. I know others who spent up to sixty days. Avoid the thirty-day marathons for your first time. Best to start out too short and want to do it again, rather than too long and never want to go back.

Life is a sticky business, so reserve a block of time and prepare to cut the cords of responsibility. Get your life in order, so you are not worrying whether or not the bills are paid rather than contemplating the meaning of life. The older you get the harder it becomes to cut the cords. Few students realize the luxury of time the college age provides. One's twenties are a window of opportunity for the grand adventure of spiritual seeking.

Where to go is the next consideration. It is best to not even see another person for the duration. Dining with others, or listening to singing and chanting as at some monastic centers is distracting. There are options besides retreat centers, maybe a friend or friend of a friend with land where you could pitch a tent. Parks and National Forests are possibilities. I know people who simply holed up in a cheap motel room for the weekend. Though tempting, using your own home is difficult, as there are many reminders of your life in the everyday world, disturbances by friends or family, and distracting temptations like the refrigerator.

Wherever you go, plan for simplicity. Food preparation can become a time-consuming chore and major distraction. Fasting is worth a try. Over-eating will make you sleepy, as will lack of exercise. The more primitive your housing situation, the more planning it takes to keep things simple: how will you cook, clean, use the toilet?

Beware of too broad a focus for your isolation. Do not plan to read ten books in two days. Or plan to decide on a career, a mate, and discover the source of thoughts. Plan a major thrust for your isolation and let all other actions support that goal.

So you found a reason, a place to go, and a plan. Now you are there, so what are the unexpected hurdles? Typically, people find reasons to leave. You decide isolation was a stupid idea, or you are not prepared, or now is not the best time, you feel weak or sick, you have too much nervous energy (cannot focus), or there is some "emergency" at home. My advice is to not shorten your isolation. If you said you would stay a week, stay a week. However, use your best judgment. Once, I meditated so long that my knees hurt day and night, but I kept changing my sitting style to continue. Adapt the details of your plan in mid-stream if necessary to preserve the whole.

Lastly, you will discover the need to...

12. Learn to tread water:

When you are depressed and despairing, do not give up and swim back to shore. Learn to tread water till inspiration arrives, which it surely will. Treading water also means not sabotaging your store of energy. Think of someone who trains for weeks for a big event, but then doubts descend and they run from the stress by staying up all night partying. Their momentum is damaged and their goal is out of focus.

Never make a decision when in a mood. By "mood," I mean the common term as in "I'm in a mood," or "he's feeling moody." A person in a mood has a negative view on practically everything. Richard Rose described it as a clouded glass. Such clouded states of perception may linger for hours or days.

"Never make a decision in a mood" is a guideline that served me well. It kept me from abandoning commitments and taking actions that led to a change in priorities.

You need a certain level of awareness about your self in order to recognize a mood, to remember your mental state before the mood, and recognize your current state. Also, you need the faith that your mood will return to its typical state. Do not take my word, observe your self in action.

What do you do while waiting for the mood to change? Keep your present commitments as best as you can. Procrastinate important decisions until the mood lifts. Tread water rather than start swimming in the direction a mood sends you.

Not all moods are negative. Sometimes we feel full of power and potential and our excitement in beginning a new undertaking is barely contained. The only potential downside is if you find yourself committing to projects in moods of inspiration, then dropping them. A little honesty will reveal whether or not you are a victim of certain positive moods.

The worst feedback loop I encountered was that of fatigue and depression. Nothing brought my spiritual search to a standstill faster. When depression hit, I got tired. If I got tired, I got depressed because I had little physical energy. One fed upon the other until I was reduced to a soggy heap which barely got out of bed. I felt like I was drowning in negativity. Besides treading water, I developed a couple of tactics to deal with this sort of depression.

Take a break. By that, I mean simply put down the book, get out of bed, stand up from meditation, or relax. Take a walk, go to a movie, go out to dinner, or simply go someplace else. They key is to not take a break for too long. A day of relaxation may become a week and then a month.

Being around friends is another helpful tactic. I wanted no one around when depressed—an unfortunate reaction to depression and the opposite of what is needed. This is when it is helpful to have a spiritual group of friends who, while they may go out for a beer with you, will not offer the temptation of getting drunk every night.

There is a second type of depression, which descends on some people like a shadow with no cause. When asked why they are depressed or what triggered it, they find no answer. I used to think they simply were not aware of the cause, but now I suspect a medical reason. There is a chemical imbalance whose trigger is not a psychological event. A switch flips and they plunge into depression.

These people should seek out a good doctor—someone who will find the right amount of medicine to control their depression, yet not take the fire out of their desire. The patient, too, must help determine what level of medicine works for them. I know one person who took slivers of a single pill because, through experimentation, that worked for them.

* * *

Some of these principles may not resonate with you and that's okay. If I were stuck on a mental desert island, and could only take one aid with me, I'd chose "practice honesty." That is the North Star that guides you to discover, adapt, and amplify all the other principles.

Acknowledgements

"Why are you on the [spiritual] path?" asked Augie.
"Because he is," he said, pointing to the guy next to me.
"And why is he on the path?"
"Because I am," I said.

Not much in life gets done without help. "The Sangha is the matrix in which the law of the ladder bears fruit," said Richard Rose. That said, what follows are my thanks to the many who have helped me along the way.

Cecy Rose, at richardroseteachings.com, for permission to quote from her husband's work, and her tireless support of his dreams.

August Turak, at augustturak.com, whose work with the Self Knowledge Symposium awoke me from a deep slumber and changed my life.

My SKS friends: Eric, Doug, Alex, William, Georg, Belle, Marcus, Sharon, Laura, Danny, Andrew, and many others who passed through the doors of 345 Harrelson Hall. These are the people who helped me learn to become a real friend.

The "Farm crew": Art T., Michael C., Bob F., Dave W., and others who I met while living at Mr. Rose's farm and chasing crazy dreams of enlightenment along with stray goats.

The TAT Foundation, at tatfoundation.org, and all those who for the past decades have kept that group alive and a beacon for finding friends on the spiritual path.

The "Book crew": Denise L., Jim L., Ricky C., Bob C., Beau B., Larry I., and my wife Aimée for providing invaluable feedback on *Subtraction*. Luke R. and Jimmy S. for help with the cover and interior design.

And to you, friend on the path.

31597326R00148

Printed in Great Britain
by Amazon